It took me many years to understand what Dr. Shih points out so well in this book. You can master biomedicine, but if you ignore the biopsychosocial and spiritual aspects of your patient's life, you will not achieve the goal of becoming a "good physician".

Ron J. Anderson, M.D.
Professor of Internal Medicine,
University of Texas Southwestern Medical Center
President and Chief Executive Officer,
Parkland Health & Hospital System

A well written book with both factual and practical information about life in medical school, intertwined with solid theological discussion. The chapter on "the good doctor" ought to be required reading for every Christian in Medicine. What an excellent reminder of why most of us became doctors to begin with.

Jean A. Wright. M.D., M.B.A.
Clinical Associate Professor of Pediatrics,
Emory University
Medical Director,
Egleston Children's Hospital at Emory University

After thirty years in a medical school environment, I finally have a book in hand that gives biblical guidance and wisdom to the pre-professional as well as graduate medical men and women. A powerful, practical book like this will change the face of medicine because it gets at the heart. Buy it, read it, and give it out liberally.

Donald K. Wood, M.D.
Chief, Surgical Services,
VA Chicago Health Care Systems, West Side Division
Associate Professor of Surgical Oncology,
University of Illinois at Chicago
Former President,
Christain Medical & Dental Society

PREPARING
FOR A
CAREER
IN
MEDICINE

Kent Shih

PAUL TOURNIER INSTITUTE

The Paul Tournier Institute is the educational division of the Christian Medical & Dental Society. The Paul Tournier Institute sponsors conferences and creates resource tools developed to help physicians, dentists, and other healthcare professionals investigate and discuss how the world of faith can be integrated with the world of biomedicine.

The Christian Medical & Dental Society is a professional society of physicians, dentists, and allied healthcare professionals. It also provides a variety of ministries to the healthcare professional including student ministries, marriage growth conferences, short-term domestic and foreign missionary opportunities, medical ethics statements, and personal mentoring. The aim of CMDS is to change the face of healthcare by changing the hearts of doctors. For more information about CMDS call 1-423-844-1000 or write CMDS at P.O. Box 7500, Bristol, TN 37621.

Library of Congress Catalog Card Number: 98-67821
ISBN Number: 0-9666809-0-1

Table of Contents

Foreword by Dr. C. Everett Koop 7

Introduction 9

Part I: The Background

1. Is Medical School for Me? 13

2. Balance and Priorities 35

3. Work and Time 49

Part II: The Work

4. Grades, MCAT, and Letters of Recommendation 65

5. Experience and Personal Qualities 77

Part III: The Future

6. Myths and Pitfalls of Medical School 99

7. The Good Doctor 119

Appendix 139

With heartfelt love and gratitude
to my wife Christine,
my parents Ding and Chao-yun Shih,
and to Bill Peel,
all of whom have influenced me
more than they know

Foreword
by Dr. C. Everett Koop

My service as both a practicing surgeon and as Surgeon General of the United States afforded me a comprehensive view of our nation's healthcare needs. I have served on numerous national boards and panels, provided congressional testimony, advised presidents, and led national healthcare reform programs. I have examined and addressed critical issues from heart disease and smoking to abortion and AIDS.

I have observed that our greatest need in America is not for technology, educational campaigns, or political solutions–though all of these may help.

Our greatest need in healthcare today is for competent, compassionate, and committed doctors. Doctors who will exhibit the hallmarks of professionalism, who will police themselves, and who will put the needs of patients and students above their own. These must be our frontline soldiers in the battle for health and wholeness in the United States. Today we stand in desperate need of doctors who not only know medicine, but also know how to comfort and assure patients by holding a hand or putting an arm around a shoulder. Doctors who realize that the cause of much pathology remains rooted in personal behavior and moral values. Doctors who can provide a patient with spiritual as well as physical help.

Until now, young men and women aspiring to be such doctors have lacked a comprehensive, authoritative resource to guide them toward a healthcare career. They have needed practical guidance from a Christian perspective to help prepare for the spiritual, emotional, and ethical challenges they will face, as well as make the most of the opportunities they will encounter.

This volume fills a vacuum and meets that need. I am unaware of any other source of such complete, authoritative, and helpful information for the Christian pursuing a career in healthcare. I have been a member of the Christian Medical & Dental Society for nearly fifty years. I know from firsthand experience that this ministry is dedicated to serving and equipping the next generation of Christian doctors. Over six decades of experience with Christian

Our greatest need in healthcare today is for competent, compassionate, and committed doctors. These must be our frontline soldiers in the battle for health and wholeness in the United States.

medical students make CMDS the premier source of help and hope for thousands of medical and dental students nationwide. If you have not yet joined a CMDS chapter, I urge you to do so immediately by contacting the number listed in this book. Along with this book, you will find CMDS to be one of your greatest resources as you pursue excellence, truth, and love in your career. I challenge you to set your sights high–to pursue your career as a calling–and to hold fast to the truth of Scripture and to its Author.

May God bless you as you strive to honor Him in all you do.

C. Everett Koop, M.D., Sc.D.
July 1998

One's years in college are significant because in a very real yet embryonic manner, we begin to take ownership of difficult issues in life. We take it upon ourselves, no longer looking primarily to parents or siblings, to think through hard questions that affect daily living. We wonder where God wants us and why. We wonder how it is that we get there and what the posture of our hearts should be while doing so. We struggle with difficult relationships between peers and colleagues, and yearn for intimate ones with fellow believers and/or a spouse. And ultimately, we ask the honest and most difficult questions before God, and do so at a depth never dealt with before in our early teen years: Who am I and who is God?

This book begins to deal with a few of these issues. It is not an answer key and does not deliver neat equations that can be plugged into life, nor is it a cookbook that has simple lists to follow which promise success. Although it does have practical suggestions for surviving the premedical years academically as well as spiritually, it is primarily a journal of sorts from me, a first-year resident, to you, a premed undergraduate. It articulates what has been on my heart and mind for years—what has kept me up at night, what has made me burn with anger, leap for joy, and cry with sorrow during the past decade or so of my life. It is my hope that at times while reading it that you will put the book down because something about it *troubles* you. Troubling thoughts are good—they spur us on to think through what needs to be clarified in our lives. It would be the greatest compliment if as a result of this book that you too should burn with anger, leap for joy, and cry with sorrow as you work out in your heart and mind very important issues.

If you are just starting college, then you are about to embark upon a very exciting journey! You might be thinking that a career in medicine is one of many options. Or you may have already started college in a non-premedical field but now find yourself thinking of changing majors and wondering what is out there. In fact, you might be considering premed as a major. Or you might even be well into your premedical years but have questions about the application process to and life during medical school. Wherever you are academically, you need to have a vision of your calling and see the big picture. You also need to employ strategies

You need to have a vision of your calling and see the big picture. You also need to employ strategies that will enable you to be successful.

9

that will enable you to be successful. This book will deal with these things.

The first three chapters of this book deal with background issues: Is medical school and a career in medicine for you? If so, what are the key concepts to guard well in your life while you pursue medicine—concepts like priorities, balance, and time management? These first three chapters are perhaps the most difficult to work through because they raise *issues of the heart.* These chapters will provoke some thought. I have learned time and again to always deal with the heart first and the hands will usually follow. In other words, if your heart is in the right place (that is, you know who you are and what you are about) then your hands will find a way to accomplish the tasks before you. It is appropriate then to follow these first three chapters with two chapters that are the nuts-and-bolts of the premedical years, and are in fact simply *issues of the hands.* They outline suggestions for better grades, MCAT scores, and interviews at medical schools. Two final chapters offer a glimpse ahead and address life and times in medical school and beyond. I will debunk some myths and address potential pitfalls in medical school as well as examine in light of Scripture what a good doctor really is.

It is my heartfelt prayer that you may gain as much from reading this book as I did from writing it. Lessons and concepts take a higher meaning when one has to teach them; however, they have the most meaning when one begins to live them. In this, perhaps you and I are both at the beginning. Let us take courage and walk boldly, knowing that the God of peace will equip us "with everything good for doing his will, and may he work in us what is pleasing to him, through Jesus Christ, to whom be glory for ever and ever" (Heb. 13:21).

Part I
The Background

Chapter 1
Is Medical School for Me?

He who chooses the beginning of a road chooses the place it leads to. It is the means that determine the end.
—Harry Emerson Fosdick

A t some point the question arises in every serious Christian's mind: Does God have a specific plan for me? For every single person, the answer is an emphatic *yes!* As we examine Scripture, we will see that first, God has gifted each one uniquely and that second, He consciously uses these unique gifts in His specific and splendid plan for our lives.

God has created each one of us distinctively. We are not the result of a cosmic accident (a theory suggested by naturalism) but the design of a divine Creator. God has formed us in such a manner that even before we were born, He knew who we were going to be and what He desired for us to do. He consciously and actively wove our makeup—our thoughts, desires, tendencies, talents, and dreams—with His purpose in mind. King David put it this way:

> O LORD, you have searched me and you know me. You know when I sit and when I rise; you perceive my thoughts from afar. You discern my going out and my lying down; you are familiar with all of my ways. Before a word is on my tongue you know it completely, O LORD. . . . For you created my inmost being; you knit me together in my mother's womb. I praise you because I am fearfully and wonderfully made. (Ps. 139:1-4, 13-14)

The image of God David portrayed is one of someone who actively and knowingly fashions His creation: "For you created my inmost being; you knit me together in my mother's womb." The image of knitting reflects labor, detail, and purpose. Knitting a sweater, or any other garment for that matter, is a laborious task, often taking weeks to finish small parts. It is a task that requires its creator to pay strict attention to detail: one missed stitch and the entire garment can be ruined. The result of such sensitive tending is a garment that has a purpose, an ultimate function to serve besides being simply ornamental. It will keep someone warm. So it is with God knitting our makeup together. He spends whatever time is necessary to finish the project; He pays great attention to every detail of our being and He intends for this great work of art to serve a function.

However, God does not stop with just initially forming who we are. Rather, throughout life, He knows His children's hearts intimately. David goes on to say, "You perceive my thoughts from afar. You discern my going out and my lying down. Before a word is on my tongue you know it completely." God not only *knows* His children's hearts but He *forms* and *shapes* them. David wrote, "Delight yourself in the LORD and he will give you the desires of your heart" (Ps. 37:4). He knows our thoughts, our desires, our talents, and our dreams because He formed them before we were born.

Let us reiterate this principle as we see how God called Jeremiah:

> The word of the LORD came to me, saying, "Before I formed you in the womb I knew you, and before you were born I set you apart; I have appointed you a prophet to the nations." "Ah, Sovereign LORD," I said, "I do not know how to speak; I am only a child." But the LORD said to me, "Do not say, 'I am only a child.' You must go to everyone I send you to and say whatever I command you." (Jer. 1:4-7)

Again, God is being clear in letting His children know that before eternity past, He formed our being and appointed to us a destiny. In Jeremiah's case, God formed in Jeremiah the abilities of a prophet and appointed that he be God's spokesman. God knew of these talents, though Jeremiah himself did not or could not see them. Jeremiah was not putting on a false cloak of humility by saying, "I do not know how to speak"; he truly believed that he did not have the talent within himself to perform the task. God, however, knew what He had created: "Do not say, 'I am only a child.' You must go to everyone I send you to and say whatever I command you." He knew the makeup of Jeremiah and his abilities—because He put them there in the first place! God knows, God forms, and God appoints.

Highlight #1

God designed each one uniquely.

What then of this "appointment," this "destiny" that God has called us, like Jeremiah, to? Can He deal with His children harshly and doom them to a future of trouble? No. While we will encounter troubles along with the rest of mankind, God purposes a future for us not of despair but of hope. One sees an example of this tenderness as God speaks through Jeremiah to the captives of Babylon.

"For I know the plans that I have for you," declares the Lord, "plans to prosper you and not to harm you, plans to give you a hope and a future." (Jer. 29:11)

Does God not intend such promises for all of His children? Or are these promises limited only to those who first heard them in Babylon? Certainly He extends such a hope for you and me. God is a benevolent God who cherishes His children. He purposes to use everything He has gifted us with, including our makeup, for His glory and for our good. Paul stated this truth in his letter to the Romans:

And we know that in all things God works for the good of those who love him, who have been called according to his purpose. For those God foreknew he also predestined to become conformed to the likeness of his Son, that he might be the firstborn among many brothers. And those he predestined, he also called; those he called, he also justified; those he justified, he also glorified. (Rom. 8:28-30)

We should have confidence in life that all things, including who we are—our thoughts, actions, dreams, and desires—work together for good. What, specifically, is the "good"? This is revealed in verse 29—that we might "become conformed to the likeness of his Son." That is a fancy way of saying that we will become more and more Christlike, inwardly and outwardly. All things work so that we should become like Christ and in doing so we will glorify God by reflecting His image, His likeness to others. We have been created by God for God. Paul puts it this way to the church at Ephesus.

Highlight #2

God will use our uniqueness in His specific and splendid plan for our lives.

For it is by grace you have been saved, through faith—and this not from yourselves, it is the gift of God—not by works, so that no one can boast. For we are God's workmanship, created in Christ Jesus to do good works, which God prepared in advance for us to do. (Eph. 2:8-10)

We are *God's workmanship,* created for good works which God has prepared beforehand. Our lives were created to reflect His goodness, His glory, His workmanship, His purpose, and not our own. Every nook and cranny of our makeup is to be used for our good and His glory—the two are inseparable. We are each unique and God will use this uniqueness in His plan for our lives—which is to reflect His glory. The purpose of our life, of our very existence, is to bring glory to Him. *This* ultimately is His specific and splendid plan for our lives.

Form Follows Function

"Form follows function" is a powerful concept that must be understood. We have established that God has designed us uniquely for His glory and our good. How exactly that works itself out is dependent upon what He designed us to be. Here is an example: oxygen is carried by hemoglobin and plays a crucial role in delivery of gases to and from tissues. Without a functional hemoglobin molecule, life would be impossible. Its role in the web of life is one that only hemoglobin can perform. Lysozyme cannot do what hemoglobin does. Neither can thrombin or calmodulin. Only hemoglobin can carry oxygen from the lungs to tissues and carbon dioxide from tissues to the lung. And this is why: hemoglobin contains heme, which is made up of four pyrrole rings linked by methene bridges and an iron molecule right in the middle. This heme group is cradled by a complicated three-dimensional network of a- and b-helices.

There also exist a number of other groups and subgroups that all work in tandem so as to stabilize and enable an oxygen molecule to bind at the center of the hemoglobin. This complex three-dimensional structure not only allows gas transport but also enables the molecule to be responsive to the changing environment—again, a property unique to hemoglobin. Every helix and subgroup plays a role in this. No part of the molecule is extraneous. For instance, should carbon dioxide levels rise and pH fall, part of this special molecule's structure is responsible for the release of oxygen. That is, as rapidly metabolizing tissue releases acid and carbon dioxide as by-products, hemoglobin senses the changing milieu and releases oxygen to the tissues so that the overworked tissues can make more energy via the electron transport system. Hemoglobin is a dynamic and responsive molecule that

The complex weave of interests, desires, dreams, gifts, and talents that God has designed within you serves a specific purpose in God's plan for your life.

How do I know what God has designed me to be?

How do I know what my specific structure or form is?

How do I know that my God-given design fits with the medical profession?

Highlight #3

Form follows function.

performs its task superbly and it does so simply because of its structure, its form.

So it is with our work. What we are to be is a function of how we are designed. Put another way, the job we will be best at and most happy with is the job that is most consistent with who we are. *Form follows function.* The complex weave of interests, desires, dreams, gifts, and talents that God has designed within you serves a specific purpose in God's plan for your life. Just as every surface residue and helix chain facilitates hemoglobin in performing its task, so your unique design facilitates performing the job God will give you.

You may ask, How do I know what God has designed me to be? How do I know what my specific structure or form is? These questions are answered through time as you begin to get a feel for what your true qualities are. There are a number of personality tests in the general market that can help you, but the basic questions that you must ask yourself are:

Where are my strengths? My weaknesses?

What do I daydream about? What am I excited about?

What have my friends, teachers, and parents told me I am good at?

Do I like to work with my hands mostly? My mind?

Do I think abstractly or concretely?

Am I patient or do I like to see immediate results?

What subjects in school am I best at? Which ones do I like the most (not necessarily the same)?

Qualities of a Medical Student

The next most reasonable question is: How do I know that my God-given design fits with the medical profession? I would answer in two ways. First, there is no way of knowing with absolute assurance until and unless one becomes a part of the profession. Very few premedical students have a very good idea what the medical profession is really like; most choose their careers based on more of a hunch. As Christians, however, we have the confidence of knowing that ultimately God is in control and that "in all things God works for the good of those who love him" (Rom. 8:28). Although we cannot be assured that medicine is the best job for us, we can proceed in life with confidence, trusting that "the LORD will guide [us] always" (Isa. 58:11).

Second, medicine is broad enough to fit many types of people. There are a number of different fields within medicine that can accommodate a wide range of personalities. It is not true, however, that just anybody can be a good doctor. There are a few qualities that I believe all successful medical students must have.

Quality #1
Successful medical students are motivated by love.

The most-quoted reason for wanting to go to medical school is, "I want to help people." Although it sounds trite and simplistic, it is still the best answer. The medical profession hungers for idealistic young men and women who genuinely care about people, feel they can make a difference in people's lives, and find contentment in doing so. This ideal is called love. Paul underscored the importance of love in his first letter to the Corinthians:

> If I speak in the tongues of men and of angels, but have not love, I am only a resounding gong or a clanging cymbal. If I have the gift of prophecy and can fathom all mysteries and all knowledge, and if I have a faith that can move mountains, but have not love, I am nothing. If I give all I possess to the poor and surrender my body to the flames, but have not love, I gain nothing. . . . And now these three remain: faith, hope and love. But the greatest of these is love. (1 Cor. 13:1-3, 13)

If 1 Corinthians 13 were written today, it might read:

> If I give countless monumental speeches and lectures

The medical profession hungers for idealistic young men and women who genuinely care about people, feel they can make a difference in people's lives, and find contentment in doing so.

that move masses and shape the way they think, but do not have love, I have become a resounding gong or a clanging cymbal. And if I have the gift of leadership and preside over the American Medical Association and World Health Organization; if I have the Christian witness that gets me elected as a trustee with this Christian organization or as an elder with that church, but do not have love, I am nothing. And if I give up a six-figure salary to work in a rural health-care clinic or Third World country, but do not have love, it profits me nothing.

Paul reemphasized this concept in his letter to the churches in Galatia.

> For in Christ Jesus neither circumcision nor uncircumcision has any value. The only thing that counts is faith expressing itself through love. (Gal. 5:6)

In its proper Jewish context, circumcision was the most spiritual act you could perform. For non-Jews today, for instance, it might be having quiet times or winning souls for Jesus. Substituting these acts for the act of circumcision, the passage would read, "For in Christ Jesus neither having quiet times nor winning souls nor not having quiet times or not winning souls has any value. The only thing that counts is faith expressing itself through love."

We express that love toward people when we serve them in the manner in which Christ taught. This is not to deny that a mechanic can show love on a daily basis at work. This is to say that for all of the external rewards a physician may receive, love is the only proper motive for entering medicine. It is in fact the only proper motive for all decisions in life. It is not too idealistic; it is biblical.

Highlight #4
Successful medical students are motivated by love.

Highlight #5
Successful medical students are intellectual people.

Quality #2
Successful medical students are intelligent.

This may seem obvious, but it is important to emphasize that the intellectual pressures on a physician are high. During my first week of medical school, a physiology professor told me he calculated that medical students will have to learn an average about 150 facts per day of medical school! In fact, physicians do not stop learning after medical school; the learning really just begins there. Medical school will equip a physician for a lifetime of learning. There will always be journals and articles to read and conferences and workshops to attend. Medicine is an art that is never mastered and a field we are always discovering more about, and therefore one must never stop learning.

Quality #3
Successful medical students are fascinated by the biological processes of life.

A popular reductionistic worldview states that a human being is no more than just a bag of organs. Some Christians, on the other hand, emphasize the belief that humans are principally spiritual beings and only secondarily physical beings. The truth is it is impossible to separate the spiritual and the physical components of an individual; he or she is a single unit composed of both. Furthermore, it is invalid to think that there is a "secular world" and a "sacred world," that there is "regular work" and "God's work." It is all God's work. This work may or may not glorify, honor, and reflect the image of God, but whether it does or not is a function of the heart and not of the work itself.

Many have been duped by the idea that two worlds exist and the spiritual one is inherently superior to the physical. Therefore, according to this thinking, spiritual work must be inherently superior to physical work. That is, it is inherently better to spend fifteen minutes sharing your faith with someone than it is to spend fifteen minutes sewing up a laceration. This, simply put, is poor thinking. Let me say it again: there is no dichotomy between sacred and secular. We don't do "ordinary" work *or* God's work. All work being done under the sun is according to God's providential plan. He is the God of both the physical and the spiritual.

Therefore, the Christian physician must be interested in the whole person, and as such he or she is in an incredibly unique position to impact both the spiritual and the physical health of his/her patients. It is important to note that it is not "wrong" if one's interest is primarily in the spiritual component of human beings. This may be God's

Highlight #6

Christian physicians must be interested in biological processes of life (as well as in the spiritual aspect of human beings).

Highlight #7

Successful medical students find gratification in hard work.

way of calling an individual into seminary and ultimately to become a pastor or minister of some sort. However, a Christian physician must be interested in the whole person—spiritual and physical—to truly honor God.

You must have a basic (if not consuming) interest in the biological processes of life. It would be absurd for an individual to spend countless years of his life learning about ATP, ascites and ampicillin, biotin, biliary cirrhosis, bisacodyl, and so on, when there is no fundamental interest in God's wonderful creation—the human body. There is an intricacy and wonder about its design that captures the imagination and astounds even the harshest of atheists. Life is simply too short to work in a field one does not and cannot love.

Quality #4
Successful medical students find gratification in hard work.

Medical students and residents sometimes work eighty- to one-hundred-hour weeks, borrow tens or hundreds of thousands of dollars, and earn minimum wage for years, all while their high-school and college friends are having families and making a living. One of the reasons they are able to continue without becoming callous or cynical is because they *enjoy hard work*. Work is not simply tolerated—it is anticipated. There is something about the process of work that is immeasurably rewarding. Solomon, wise and experienced, said:

> It is good and proper for a man to eat and drink, and to find satisfaction in his toilsome labor under the sun during the few days of life God has given him—for this is his lot. Moreover, when God gives any man wealth and possessions, and enables him to enjoy them, to accept his lot and be happy in his work—this is a gift of God. He seldom reflects on the days of his life, because God keeps him occupied with gladness of heart. (Eccl. 5:18-20)

Understand the context of Solomon's words. He wrote Ecclesiastes near the end of his life. It is a message of perspective and reflection. No longer the young romantic as when he wrote Song of Songs, neither was he the ambitious visionary empire-builder described in 1 Kings. He had achieved and experienced far more in his lifetime than you or I could even imagine! And yet, near the end of his life, he charged those behind him not to give their lives to overambitious or overromantic pursuits but rather to work hard and enjoy the fruits of labor. He challenged his readers to lead a simple life and enjoy basic pleasures like work and food.

This is a difficult concept to reconcile in our success-driven society. We "need" to be doctors or lawyers. We "need" to have the perfect boyfriend/girlfriend, or the perfect spouse and the perfect kids. Even our Christian subculture is success-driven. The spiritual treadmill can be more exhausting than any other. We "need" to be Bible-study leaders, disciplers of men and women, soul-winning zealots. We "need" to be having thirty-minute quiet times, writing prayer journals, and articulating perfect testimonies. Solomon had at one time all of these things and more, yet his conclusion was essentially that the reward is the labor itself—not the money, fame, or impact that labor brings. Successful medical students don't look for gratification five, ten, or fifteen years down the road; they find it just where they are, in the work they're doing today.

Get a Glimpse into the Future

Typically, the average premedical student has a superficial understanding of the true life of a physician. In retrospect, I can see how clueless I was! Still, there exist windows of opportunity to see what life may hold if you pursue a medical degree. The following are some of the keyholes into which you may peer for a more accurate picture.

Physicians remember all too well their own years in training.

Glimpse #1
Talk to private physicians.

I have never met a physician who was unwilling to answer tough questions regarding medicine. Some, in fact, may graciously offer to bring you in to see patients on a periodic basis. Take advantage of that, for as the Proverb says, "He who walks with the wise grows wise" (Prov. 13:20). Here are some questions you may want to ask; don't be timid—physicians remember all too well their own years in training.

- What prompted you to go into medicine?
- What changes have occurred in medicine since then?
- What do you appreciate about the field? What do you dislike?
- What do you like/dislike about the specialty you are in?
- What is your life like as a physician?
- What do you feel are the most important qualities a physician should have?
- What would you have done differently if you could have?
- What is the most important thing you wish you could pass on to the next generation of physicians.

Highlight #8

Ask medical students, residents, and attending physicians detailed questions, and read broadly about their work.

Glimpse #2
Talk to medical students and residents.

Contact the dean of students at a local medical school and ask for several names of students and/or residents who may be open to talking to a prospective medical student. Then, do the same as you would with the private physicians. Remember to judge their words by their actions. (Some students and residents may have a martyr's complex and like for you to believe that they have not slept, eaten, or used the bathroom in ten days! As we will discuss later, this isn't necessarily so.)

Glimpse #3
Read biographies, books, and articles by physicians.

A tremendous window into the life of a physician is literature written by a physician. Not only can the tome enlighten the mind, it can inspire the soul. Take advantage of resources such as Paul Brand's *Fearfully and Wonderfully Made* and Ben Carson's *Gifted Hands*. Tom Hale's books, including *Don't let the Goat Eat the Loquat Tree*, give an honest perspective of the missionary doctor's life and struggles.

Glimpse #4
Get involved with Christian Medical and Dental Society-Premed.

There exists a valuable and creative opportunity to gain insight into the life of a Christian physician within this unique resource. Students in CMDS-Premed have historically spent time with Christian physicians over meals, in the hospital, and even overseas on missions trips. They also participate in CMDS national student conventions and regional meetings. Furthermore, students meet monthly to fellowship and hear speakers on topics that range from ethics to time management to the how to's of medical school. The relationships and networking that develop from such a resource may prove beneficial throughout your life. If you do not have such a student organization at your school but would like to know more about it, or about initiating a chapter at your school, refer to the Appendix of this book.

Words for Women

When I was in college, I was part of a small study group. There were four or five of us who had the same declared major, took most of the same science classes, and worked in research labs in or around the same area. I seemed to never be able to get away from them! Actually, many of them are good friends that I still keep in touch with and expect to for life.

One particular friend, "Jennifer," maintained a fabulous grade-point average and participated in extracurricular activities and research projects. Yet she was always extraordinarily noncommittal about the prospects of medical school. It seemed to me at the time that if one *could* get into medical school, then one certainly *should* go. My argument was reasonable enough: medicine is such a broad and diverse profession that one can always find some specialty or subspecialty that will suit one's temperament and gifts. When Jennifer finally decided not to go to medical school, I was so baffled and almost outraged at the thought of such lost opportunity that I confronted her about it. *What could she possibly be thinking? Does she even know what she is turning down?* It turned out that in fact she did know and she had been thinking about the decision far longer and far more deeply than I had realized.

Since that time, I have noticed that for many women the decision to pursue medicine is a delicate matter. On the one hand, many women find that their skills and personalities are suited for medicine—they are smart, compassionate, and hardworking. Furthermore, a select subset of society, friends, and perhaps even family members reinforce in the minds of these very talented women that to be "successful" they must be in a high-paying, specialized, and recognized field—like medicine. And so the decision seems a good one.

On the other hand, however, these same women know that they desire, if not now then certainly at a later date, a marriage and family to build and nurture. They also understand the demands and rigors of training and practicing and do not see how the two are compatible. To complicate matters, there may be another subset of society and group of loved ones who perpetuate the belief that women are most "successful" if they place an emphasis on their home life and sacrifice their professions. The issue creates a terrible angst for many women in college.

Highlight #9

For many women, the decision to pursue medicine is a delicate matter.

As I have never had to deal with this issue personally, I certainly cannot claim to be an authority on the issue. I have, however, spoken with several women at various stages of life who have faced the issue. These comments are intended to serve as a cross-section of opinions. There is no one "right answer"; the right answer is found in the context of your own life through much prayer, wisdom, and diligence.

"Sarah" is a thirty-one-year-old married mother of one who practiced general pediatrics for one year, then stopped to be a full-time mom. She writes honestly:

> There are many seasons of life—all of which are under God's sovereign control. I grew up loving science and by the fifth grade I knew that I wanted to be a doctor. However, my motivation for entering medicine was not solely based on that. Upon reflecting over this past year, I realized that part of why I entered medicine was performance-based. That is, I fell into the trap of believing that I would be better off—more respected, more loved, and more happy—if

I was a "successful doctor." I felt that I would be letting my family and friends down if I did not enter medicine. This year off has helped me see that.

On the other hand, there were experiences in medical school and residency training that I would not trade for the world. The hardships of those years yielded a strength of character and seasoning of faith. I saw firsthand the goodness of God extended to me despite myself—I came to a deeper understanding of God's grace. In addition, I now have obtained a skill that can be used for a lifetime. I still enjoy pediatrics and desire to practice it again in some context. I know that I will never do it full-time again as I believe that God's idea of balance in my life does not include that, but I can envision part-time or short-term opportunities in the future that can be used for His glory and my good.

"Laura" is thirty-five, married, a mother of two, and a general surgeon. She writes knowingly:

Your interests and priorities will change with time. You may not know when and what they will be, but if you realize they will change and you will admit change as it happens, your life will be better. As a wife, general surgeon, and mother of two, my obligations are far different from those I faced as a single medical student. I never envisioned myself as a general surgeon before my fourth year of medical school. I chose that specialty after I quit listening to conventional wisdom and realized that God made me a woman with special abilities and talents that were suited to performing surgery. As I went through surgical residency as a single person, I was able to travel to a mission hospital where I worked closely with a missionary surgeon. What a great role model for me, as a Christian and as a surgeon.

During the years after my residency, my life as a surgeon changed dramatically with marriage and then children. I am blessed as a physician to have an intimate role with people who are afraid and/or sick. No other career would have given me that physical and emotional intimacy. But through the years, the exact nature of my practice has been altered and will be altered to meet my priorities at home. It is some-times overwhelming and very demanding, but I am intellectually and spiritually challenged and fulfilled. My advice to young women is, of course, to seek in prayer where God would have you. Then assess your talents and the ability that He has given you and use them where you would fit most naturally.

"Christine" is a twenty-eight-year-old married student. She was a premed major in college but decided against medical school, opting instead for nurse-practitioner school. She writes:

Sometimes, big decisions in life are simply "backed into." The career decision was an especially difficult one for me, requiring much prayer, consideration, and a careful sifting of others' opinions. I felt that at the age of twenty-three it was simply too late in life to make a long and inflexible commitment to medicine since medical school, residency, and fellowship could potentially require anywhere from seven to fifteen years of life after college. I worked in a hospital setting for several years, during which I got married and moved to a different city. At this time I was able to evaluate different options. Most importantly, I was able to separate the truth from fiction—that is, while being a physician is a worthy pursuit for some, it was simply too demanding and inflexible for me. My goals in life and the talents God has given me would be better suited to my being a licensed family nurse practitioner.

The bottom line is, there are other viable options that do provide the opportunity to practice medicine and take care of patients, while still allowing you to maintain a family, marriage, church, and personal life. I also considered training as a physician's assistant prior to committing to FNP school. Physical and occupational therapy exist in the same genre of professions, though I did not seriously consider these. All make a reasonable annual salary ($50,000 to $80,000, some even as high as $100,000). The proverbial "straw that broke the camel's back" for me came when a female friend who was a resident told me that she would not have gone to medical school but chosen FNP or PA school instead if she had known about other options earlier in her life. She said that God could use her in all the same ways in patients' lives in these professions while still giving her the time and energy to spend at home when the day was over. God can and does call women into medicine; He also calls women into other professions. The key is to explore your options.

There is no doubt in my mind that these comments reveal but the tip of the iceberg of issues for women who are deciding about medical school. But I hope that these women's comments are enlightening and spur some thought, questions, and prayer.

Highlight #10
The key is to explore your options.

Housekeeping

Part of the process of making a decision about medical school involves what I call "housekeeping." This means making choices about lifestyle issues: what hours, income, and specialties you prefer.

The average physician can expect to work anywhere from forty to eighty hours per week. Physicians are also "on call," which means that no matter where they are, a beeper may summon their aid or presence if a problem arises with one of their patients. Often these problems can be solved with a phone call; other times, the physician will have to go in to the hospital or office. Average "call" hours number between about twenty and forty. The following weekly calender is representative of some physicians' workweeks (obviously, some work more and some less).

The average salary of a physician in 1995 was $143,000.[1] There is, of course, much

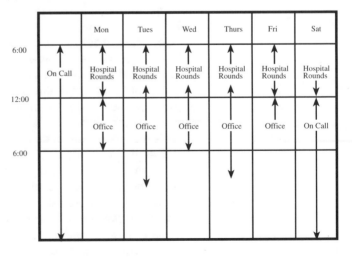

29

variability within that average. Primary-care physicians in small rural towns may make only $30,000 per year while some subspecialty surgeons may make well over $500,000 per year. Generally, primary-care specialists (family practitioners, internal medicine specialists, and pediatricians) make between $90,000 and $250,000 while surgical specialties make between $140,000 to $350,000.[2] Academic physicians make less than private physicians, but the challenge and reward of research and teaching make it more appealing to them. In addition, academic physicians enjoy a more flexible schedule as they have more control over their day; they do not necessarily work any less, but they can generally come and go as they please.

Below is a profile of specialties and the kind of work each involves. A graphic representation of various aspects of their fields follows. These data were compiled in 1991 from a survey of almost three thousand physicians spanning thirty specialties.[3]

Anesthesiology manages pain and stress during surgical, obstetrical, and some medical procedures and provides life support under the stress of anesthesia and surgery.

Emergency medicine focuses on recognition and care of patients who are acutely ill or injured. It is often diverse, broad-based, and technical in nature.

Family practice focuses on care of the whole family. As such, family physicians can deliver services across the entire spectrum of care regardless of patient age, sex, or condition.

General surgery is "the mother of surgical subspecialties." General surgery today usually involves gastrointestinal surgery. Subspecialties include colon and rectal, neurological, ophthalmological, orthopedic, otolaryngological, plastics (reconstruction and cosmetics), cardiothoracic, and urologic.

Internal medicine specialists diagnose and treat a broad spectrum of acute and chronic illnesses, as well as help to promote health and prevent disease. Subspecialties in internal medicine include, among others, allergists, cardiologists, dermatologists, endocrinologists, gastroenterologists, hematologists, infectious-disease specialists, oncologists, and neurologists.

Obstetrics focuses on care before, during, and after

a woman gives birth. **Gynecology** treats diseases and provides preventative care for the female reproductive system.

 Pathology focuses on the causes, manifestations, and diagnoses of disease. The physician in this field often functions as a consultant, applying a range of basic sci-

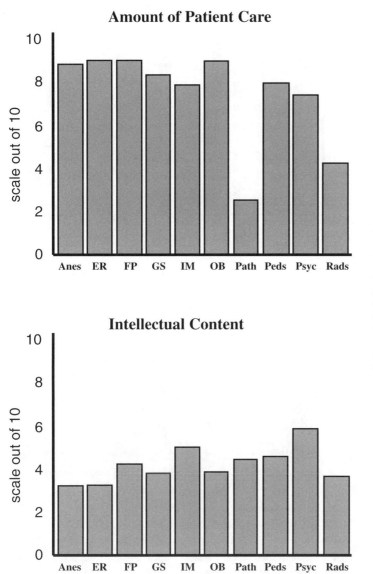

Amount of Patient Care

scale out of 10

Anes ER FP GS IM OB Path Peds Psyc Rads

Anes = Anesthesiology
ER = Emergency Room medicine
FP = Family Practice
GS = General Surgery
IM = Internal Medicine
OB = Obstetrics and Gynecology
Path = Pathology
Peds = Pediatrics
Psyc = Psychiatry
Rads = Radiology

Intellectual Content

scale out of 10

Anes ER FP GS IM OB Path Peds Psyc Rads

ences to diagnose the disease.

Pediatric doctors diagnose and treat infants, children, adolescents, and young adults, counsel patients and

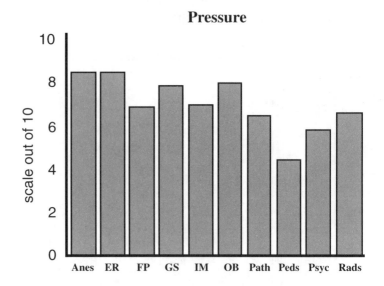

Pressure

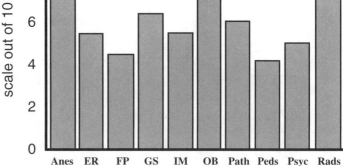

Income

Anes = Anesthesiology
ER = Emergency Room medicine
FP = Family Practice
GS = General Surgery
IM = Internal Medicine
OB = Obstetrics and Gynecology
Path = Pathology
Peds = Pediatrics
Psyc = Psychiatry
Rads = Radiology

their parents, and provide preventative care.

Psychiatry involves the diagnosing and treatment of mental, emotional, and behavioral disorders using discussion and various drugs if necessary.

Radiology involves the diagnosis and treatment of disease using X rays and other forms of radiant energy; it is now largely a consultative role.

Points to Ponder

1. Discuss the passages we read in Psalm 139 and Jeremiah 1. How intimately does God know us?

2. Based on the passages we read in Romans 8:28-30 and Ephesians 2:8-10, what is the chief role of man?

3. Consider the passage we read in 1 Corinthians 13. List some "good" things that are devoid of love. Share them with the group.

4. Besides love, what are some motivations, both proper and improper, for going to medical school?

5. Reread the passage in Ecclesiastes 5:18-20. Why is it difficult to "find satisfaction in . . . toilsome labor"? How can you apply Solomon's advice?

6. What are your current impressions of the medical profession? Of the physician's lifestyle? How do you fit into these pictures?

7. What specialty field interests you?

Notes

1. Merritt, Hawkins and Associates, *1995-1996 Physician Recruitment Incentives* (Irvine, CA: Merritt, Hawkins and Assoc.), 2-3.

2. Ibid.

3. *Glaxo Evaluation Pathway Program: Specialty Profiles* (Research Triangle Park, NC: Glaxo, Inc., 1991).

Chapter 2
Balance and Priorities

I have never let my schooling interfere with my education.
—Mark Twain

You can lead a boy to college, but you cannot make him think.
—Elbert Hubbard

T he decision to pursue medicine as a career is not an easy one. It should not be made quickly or lightly. The process of deciding is laborious and can take months, even years. Moreover, once you have made the decision to pursue medical school, the road to entrance is in most cases even more difficult. It will require years of dedication and discipline—strategizing, prioritizing, knuckle-grinding hard work, and sacrifice. In fact, the hardest part of the undergraduate years for me was learning to say no to so many good and rewarding opportunities because of my decision to pursue medical school. It is all worth it, however, if God is calling you into this particular field.

Before we examine the specifics about the college years, we will first discuss some general topics relevant to your undergraduate experience. The first is competition.

The Applicants Are Coming! The Applicants Are Coming!

For the last three decades, the scientific community has amassed a tremendous amount of knowledge about the biological processes of life. With this rapid progress came a perceived demand for physicians and scientists with more specialized training and indeed, a generation of researchers and specialists ensued. From 1960-1970, medical schools increased enrollment by 100 percent and even a number of medical schools were founded.[1]

The attractiveness of a medical career apparently tapered in the 1980s as both the enrollment size and applicant pool fell. In 1974, for every available spot there were 2.4 applicants. In 1988 this ratio dropped to 1.6 and the number of applicants to medical school was at an all-time low.[2]

With the dawn of a new decade, however, the applicant pool surged. In 1995, there were three applicants for each spot. That is, there were a total of 46,591 applicants to medical school for the 16,253 spots available.[3] The number of applicants is now at an all-time high. Furthermore, women and minorities have begun to enter medicine in large numbers. In 1970, only 11 percent of the applicant pool were women, compared to 42.5 percent presently.

Minority applicants now make up over 11 percent of the applicant group.[4]

Competition is stiff and the opportunity for graduate medical education is becoming increasingly difficult. These statistics are in no way meant to discourage you, but to encourage you while trusting in the sovereignty of God to use the reality of the situation as motivation toward excellence. This involves two very important topics: balance and priorities.

On one hand, many, but not all, concepts of balance are good. In their book *Balancing Life's Competing Demands*, Doug Sherman and William Hendricks helpfully liken balancing one's life to performing in a pentathlon. They explain that there are five very diverse and challenging arenas in life in which one competes, and to succeed one must be successful at all five. One event is no more important than the next; all are equally valid. The five areas they suggest are your personal life, your family, your church life, your work, and your community life. Personal life includes individual Scripture study and prayer as well as hobbies, athletics, and the like. Family life would not only include actual meaningful time spent with family members but also duties such as paying bills and fixing the sink. Church life refers to Bible study groups, church activities, and friendships. Work life describes our jobs and the relationships therein, and community life would include any civic or neighborhood duties or responsibilities we've accepted. Sherman and Hendricks exhort us to find a reasonable balance between these five areas. While daily living is not so easily compartmentalized, it's true that multiple needs and opportunities exist in our lives which warrant our time and attention, and there is no hierarchy in those needs and opportunities. All are gifts from God by which we relate to Him and this world.

On the other hand, there are concepts of balance that are not good. There is a fear that should an individual be "out of balance"—that is, have his or her priorities shifted unequally for extended periods of time—that life for this individual will be useless and unfulfilling. For instance, the undergraduate premedical regime may be viewed as an unbalanced life. Some may say a person studying for two to eight hours a day is "too focused." Once one is in medical school, though, gone are the days of "balance": juggling gymnastics, TriHiY, Young Life, student govern-

Highlight #1

Due to competition, balance and priorities become exceedingly important.

ment, football, Big Brother/Sister program, the chess club, and the part-time job. Now life consists of classes, studying, eating, and if you are lucky, a couple of hours to exercise. Many would say that this is not the balance one needs to maintain whole health. While this fear may be real enough, the problem with this thinking is that the reference point for balance is the cultural norm, not individual limits. Determining what makes up a balanced life has to take into account what the person involved is trying to achieve and what costs that will incur. Usually those costs will occur over a short term in order for the person to reach a long-term goal. Studying for two to eight hours is only "out of balance" when the norm it's compared to is studying for one to two hours per day. Balance cannot be defined by what is average for society but rather by what is normal for an individual. Each person is made differently, with a different calling in life. There must be regard for an individual's situation, gifts, temperament, and calling. In God's providential plan, the person studying six to eight hours a day may one day be the one who finds a cure for cancer or leads a nation out of an economic crisis. All of God's people play different roles.

I raise this issue because unfortunately, this myopic "out of balance" perspective seems extraordinarily present in mainstream Christian culture. There a perceived imbalance is often judged as a manifestation of misplaced priorities. Christian students are sadly viewed as "worldly" or "workaholics" once they're declared "out of balance."

Here are the facts: God may call you "out of balance," as some see it, for a period of time, as He often did His Son Jesus. Early in the book of John, Jesus traveled from the city of Aenon, where He was baptized by John the Baptist, to Galilee. However, He traveled through Sychar, a city of Samaria, where He met and ministered to an unnamed woman over a drink of water. Understand that He had traveled about thirty-five miles in windy, dusty, hot (at least 100 degrees) weather; He was hungry, thirsty, and tired. He was not what society would call "in balance." And of course, His disciples knew this as they attempted to persuade Him to "stay in balance" by offering Him nourishment. "Rabbi, eat," they begged. I can hear their pleas even now. "There is a time to work, and a time to rest. This, dear Teacher, is a time to rest!" But Jesus, as always, admonished them wisely. "My food is to do the will of Him who sent Me, and to accomplish His work." Jesus knew that the parameters of staying "in balance" were not in society's expectations of themselves or of Him, but in His Father's calling. Here Jesus was and always is in perfect balance.

Know and understand that God may call you out of proverbial "balance" during your undergraduate years. Some may criticize you for your devotion to your studies. Remember, you are not "out of balance" if God has called you to invest this time in your life toward studies. You are right where you need to be. I'm not referring here to breaking fellowship or ignoring such precious means of grace as Scripture, prayer, evangelism, and the like. I'm just encouraging you not to be fooled by rhetoric. Join a small group! Study the Word! Exercise with friends! Go out on dates! But remember—do not worship what some may call "balance"; accomplish the work that God has placed in front of you.

Priorities

A friend I'll call Charley, who was recently admitted into medical school, told me that before he could commit to medicine as a career he had to be sure that it would never be more important to him than God. He already felt that his studies consumed so much of his time and attention that in medical school it would be nearly impossible for him "keep God first." Charley bore a gnawing guilt about spending more time on "secular" things—studies—and so little time on "godly" things—Bible study, prayer, and evangelism. Because of his perceived imbalance, he felt he was near or already in the act of committing idolatry. That is, Charley felt that his studies were competing for time he should spend with God in "godly" activities.

The failure of my friend was not in his sincerity of heart but in his inability to see that God owns him entirely. According to Charley, God is to be at the top of his "list" of priorities that looks like this: 1. God; 2. Family; 3. Friends; 4. Work; 5. Ministry. However, according to God, He is not to be on the list at all. He *is* the list, in the sense that all of these things are given by Him and to be used for Him. I describe Charley's way of thinking as the *list paradigm*, where one's priorities in life are listed according to their

Highlight #2

The parameters of "balance" are not defined by society, but by God's plan for your life.

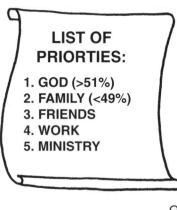

LIST OF PRIORTIES:

1. **GOD (>51%)**
2. **FAMILY (<49%)**
3. **FRIENDS**
4. **WORK**
5. **MINISTRY**

List paradigm: Lists our priorities in life, requiring that God be at least slightly more important than everyone else.

importance. Of course, one's relationship with God is the first priority. Usually, family or marriage is close behind. According to this paradigm, as long as God has the majority of our heart and interest, all will be okay—a 51 percent to 49 percent proposition. So, we must hold back the reins of our hearts on marriage, friendships, work, and whatever other priorities we have, to keep them at bay—under 50 percent—while at the same time mustering up more love for God so as to keep Him more important than all of the other things—over 50 percent. I do not believe this way of thinking is biblical. God does not want just over 50 percent of us; He wants all of us!

God's first and greatest commandment to us is clearly stated in the Bible:

> I am the LORD your God, who brought you out of Egypt, out of the land of slavery. You shall have no other gods before me. You shall not make for yourself an idol in the form of anything in heaven above or on the earth beneath or in the waters below. You shall not bow down to them or worship them; for I, the LORD your God, am a jealous God. (Deut. 5:6-9)

God is emphatic that He simply will not compete for our hearts against anything or anyone. He does not want to nudge out Number 2 in a photo finish for the blue ribbon. He wants to be the only one out of the blocks, leading us in a victory lap, a triumphal procession (2 Cor. 2:14). Let us look at how Jesus phrased this issue of priority:

> If anyone comes to me and does not hate his father and mother, his wife and children, his brothers and sisters—yes, even his own life—he cannot be my disciple. And anyone who does not carry his cross and follow me cannot be my disciple.
> Suppose one of you wants to build a tower. Will he not first sit down and estimate the cost to see if he has enough money to complete it? For if he lays the foundation and is not able to finish it, everyone who sees it will ridicule him, saying, "This fellow began to build and was not able to finish."
> Or suppose a king is about to go to war against

another king. Will he not first sit down and consider whether he is able with ten thousand men to oppose the one coming against him with twenty thousand? If he is not able, he will send a delegation while the other is still a long way off and will ask for terms of peace. In the same way, any of you who does not give up everything he has cannot be my disciple. (Luke 14:26-33)

Jesus uses strong language to point out what should be the nature of our love and commitment to God versus our love and commitment to the rest of this world. Simply put, the two do not compare. They are not even on the same level. We are not called, as some may initially think, to literally hate our parents, since God Himself commanded that we honor them (Deut. 5:16); we are to love them as an expression of our love for God. We are not to look at life with a 51 percent versus 49 percent, God-versus-world perspective, but a 100-percent-God perspective.

How, you may ask, is this possible? How is it humanly possible to love God in everything that we do? Do we have to be constantly humming praise songs or saying prayers in a mantralike fashion? Are we to be ubiquitously evangelizing every unbeliever we encounter? How is it possible to be about what Paul exhorts:

Be joyful always; pray continually; give thanks in all circumstances, for this is God's will for you in Christ Jesus. (1 Thess. 5:16-18)

I think it is possible, and without having to become a mindless, babbling religious drone looking at every moment in life as just another ritual. Before it is possible, however, I believe that we need to readjust our thinking. We must see priorities in a different light.

Gifts as a Medium of Change

I like to think of priorities in an altogether different way. Instead of the list paradigm, I like to think of priorities according to the "GIST" paradigm. GIST stands for Gifts Intended to Satisfy and Teach. All five things on Charley's list are gifts given to us by God—work included. They are

Highlight #3

God is not first on your list; He gives the list.

41

all part of God's program for us. We should not fear embracing them passionately and pursuing them tenaciously. They are inherently good. They are not intended to conflict with our relationship with God, as long as we view and use them properly.

Specifically, these gifts serve two important purposes besides being a means of providing for our physical needs. They are a medium of change in our lives and a vehicle of worship to God.

To understand the first purpose, that all things, work included, are used as a medium of change in our lives, let us again be reminded of what Paul said is the role of all of the people and events in our lives:

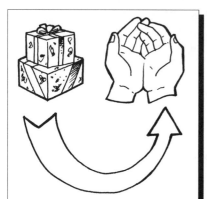

GIST paradigm: "Gifts Intended to Satisfy and Teach": gifts given by God which we use to offer worship back to Him.

And we know that in all things God works for the good of those who love him, who have been called according to his purpose. For those God foreknew he also predestined to be conformed to the likeness of his Son, that he might be the firstborn among many brothers. And those he predestined, he also called; those he called, he also justified; those he justified, he also glorified. (Rom. 8:28-30)

In other words, through our families and marriages, our jobs, our friends and associates, our ministries—God is working the purpose of our being conformed to the image of His Son Jesus. All of the things on Charley's list of priorities are given to us by God to be used as a medium of change in our lives. God will use these areas to teach us how to behave as His children as we are "conformed to the likeness of his Son." Through these areas, work included, we will learn of our need for God and for change, and as Scripture promises, God will meet our need and change our hearts.

Paul stated that difficulties in life, including those at work, are meant as a medium of change:

Not only so, but we also rejoice in our sufferings, because we know that suffering produces perseverance, character; and character, hope. And hope does not disappoint us, because God has poured out his love into our hearts by the Holy Spirit, whom he has given us (Romans 5:3-5).

James put it this way:

> Consider it pure joy, my brothers, whenever you face trials of many kinds, because you know that the testing of your faith develops perseverance. Perseverance must finish its work so that you may be mature and complete, not lacking anything. (James 1:2-4)

It is through the mundane struggles of daily living that the Christian's heart is shaped and molded, and from this heart comes the fruit of Christian character. Incidentally, it has been my experience that Christians in college have little difficulty with this fact—namely that God will use our studies and ultimately our jobs to make us into the people He wants us to be. The difficulty is in accepting the fact that He does not hurry in doing so! Young adults (myself included) want so badly for God's work in their lives to be done in a decade or less that we are blinded to the fact that He sets the pace. Yes, it is true that young Christians generally grow fast initially, but if there is to be continued steady growth, it will and must be slow.

> God Himself will modify the pace. This is important to see, since in most instances when seeming declension begins to set in, it is not, as so many think, a matter of backsliding. . . . Let's settle it once and for all—there are no shortcuts to reality! A meteor is on a shortcut as it proceeds to burn out, but not a star, with its steady light so often depended upon by navigators. Unless the time factor is acknowledged from the heart, there is always danger of turning to the false enticement of a shortcut via the means of "experiences," and "blessings," where one becomes pathetically enmeshed in the vortex of ever-changing "feelings," adrift from the moorings of scriptural facts.[5]

I recently discovered gardening as a hobby. I made it my ambition to have full, thick bushes of pepper plants, each bearing dozens or hundreds of large, shiny, pungent peppers of all sorts. I planted seeds for jalapeño, habanero, serrano, cayenne, tabasco, banana, Mongolian, and yes, bell peppers. For weeks, I did not see any growth. Finally there appeared tiny, weak sprouts. Every day I would go outside and check them, expecting some kind of change, some kind of growth. After all, I watered them, fertilized them, placed them in the full sun. I had weeded the garden, planted marigolds to ward off insects, tested the earth pH, and prepared the soil by tilling in mulch to make it loamy and loose. Much to my chagrin, for months I saw nothing but weak, pathetic, almost wilty three-inch plants. Nothing was happening—or so I thought. Although I could not see it, there was growth, but it was occurring in ways the naked eye could not perceive. Deep underground, an amazing series of events was taking place that promised the plants would one day flourish. Slowly but methodically, the plants' roots were working their way deeper and deeper, burrowing into every crack and extending themselves through every layer and sublayer of soil. From each plant's two main root shafts sprouted two more, and from these two another two, and so on. Eventually, these fragile plants were not so fragile anymore. Their root systems were sound and they could begin building leafage. No longer would a drought harm these plants; they were well established.

Then it happened. The stems, which had been laying down a meshy, fibrous network for months, turned brown, ruddy, and hard. The leaves, which were so few and dull, appeared suddenly as long, shiny, and thick. And then fruit. First as flowers, then as small peppers, then finally as the big, waxy, delicious peppers that I had wanted for so long.

So it is with our spiritual lives. We want so badly to grow that we do all the right things. We water ourselves with the Scriptures, set ourselves out in full sun with prayer, and even fertilize by involving ourselves in appropriate relationships. Yet there is not the growth on the outside that we want to see. Let me say that it is in the years, even decades of "mundane" acts of everyday living—work and the relationships at work and at home—where the roots of true spirituality grow deep. There is a wonder in even the mundane when we realize that spirituality is not found in special "experiences" but in the healthy development of everyday living and everyday working. Each day can have meaning and hope when seen from this viewpoint; we can live life and work with every ounce of intention and purpose

Highlight #4

Work serves as a medium by which God changes us.

when we know that "he who began a good work in you will carry it on to completion until the day of Christ Jesus" (Phil. 1:6).

Gifts as a Vehicle of Worship

The second purpose of these gifts is as a vehicle of worship unto Him. That is, all of the areas of our lives— family, friends, work, church—are meant to help us exalt Him in our hearts and enjoy a relationship with Him. Paul exhorted the Christians at Colossae: "Whatever you do, work at it with all your heart, as working for the Lord, not for men" (Col. 3:23).

Paul underscored an important concept here: worship is a matter of the heart and not of the hands. We do not worship God by simply tithing or singing a praise song en masse; we worship God by having a grateful heart in all we do, giving money and singing being but two of many things. We worship God by understanding and having our hearts impacted by the magnanimity of the cross. We worship God by exalting Him, by thinking greatly of Him and His deeds. It is our heart that God is interested in, not simply our hands. For "man looks at the outward appearance, but the LORD looks at the heart" (1 Sam. 16:7).

There is a common saying: "Don't put the cart before the horse." In Christendom, we often like to put the hands, figuratively speaking, before the heart. It simply won't do. The heart comes first, and the hands follow. From the wellsprings of the heart comes the work of the hands. Jesus taught that.

> By their fruit you will recognize them. Do people pick grapes from thornbushes, or figs from thistles? Likewise every good tree bears good fruit, but a bad tree bears bad fruit. A good tree cannot bear bad fruit, and a bad tree cannot bear good fruit. (Matt. 7:16-18)

Jesus uses the analogy of a fruit-bearing tree to teach that who we are inside determines what kind of things we are inclined to do on the outside. Good inside (pure) produces good outside (pure fruit); bad inside (impure) produces bad outside (impure fruit). We may try to dress up the outside but it will never affect the inside. Only by

45

changing the inside will our outside ever be truly changed. That is, only by true and good heart changes—changes in our makeup—will the works that follow also change to true and good works. Here is the caveat: He is the changer of hearts.

> God, who knows the heart, showed that he accepted them by giving the Holy Spirit to them, just as he did to us. He made no distinction between us and them, for he purified their hearts by faith. (Acts 15:8-9)

Highlight #5

Work serves as a vehicle by which we can worship God.

He changes our hearts, He purifies them. We cannot change our hearts and thus perform good works that glorify Him; only He can change us and through Him, we do these things. Jesus, in His final day with His disciples, emphasized:

> I am the vine; you are the branches. If a man remains in me and I in him, he will bear much fruit; apart from me you can do nothing. (John 15:5)

Worship is simply exalting God in our hearts and declaring that we are His children as we live as a redeemed people. Worship is not, as some may see it, just good works. Work is but one of many vehicles that God gives to us by which we may in turn worship Him and enjoy Him as we perform our duties heartily as His children, and not as men's slaves.

Points to Ponder

1. Using the pentathlon analogy, describe the time you allot to each area of life. Are the areas in balance according to God's plan for you?

2. Have you ever felt out of balance? Have you ever been told you were out of balance?

3. How can you work hard, yet keep balance?

4. Have you seen your priorities through a list or GIST paradigm?

5. Have you ever felt frustrated by Paul's exhortation to "pray unceasingly"? How can we actually do this?

6. What is your current level of frustration with work or study? How can seeing the true function of work help?

7. Have you seen God use your study or work to

change your heart? Have you ever felt impatient, wanting Him to finish His work in you more quickly?

8. How have you defined worship till now? Name instances where you may have put hands before heart.

Notes

1. *Medical School Admission Requirements 1997-98* (Washington DC: Association of American Medical Colleges, 1996), xi.

2. Ibid.

3. Ibid.

4. Ibid.

5. Miles Stanford, *The Green Letters: Principles of Spiritual Growth* (Grand Rapids, MI: Zondervan Publishing House, 1975), 13-14.

Chapter 3
Work and Time

*Whoever admits that he is too busy to improve his methods has
acknowledged himself to be at the end of his rope.
And that is always the saddest predicament which
anyone can get into.*
—J. Ogden Armour

*It is not enough to be busy; so are the ants. The question is:
What are we busy about?*
—Henry David Thoreau

H

aving established that all of God's gifts, work included, are given to change us, to help us worship God, and to help provide for our needs, let us take a closer look at the nature of work itself and its relationship to man.

It is helpful at this point to remember that God Himself is a worker and that He takes pleasure in working; He enjoyed creation. The account in Genesis 1 can be summed up in the opening words:

> "In the beginning God created the heavens and the earth. . . . And God saw that it was good." (Gen. 1:1, 10)

God works, and it brings Him much pleasure.

It is important to note that even before Adam and Eve sinned, God had ordained the institution of work for man as He commissioned Adam and Eve to cultivate and to keep the garden.

> The LORD God took the man and put him in the Garden of Eden to work it and take care of it. (Gen. 2:15)

Work, therefore, is not a necessary evil nor a result of the curse, as many would say, but a calling and a gift. God made Adam and Eve His coworkers in the garden, His co-tenders before they sinned. Therefore, work cannot be part of the curse of sin, but rather a good and perfect gift. God made man to enjoy the creative process too.

In addition to creating, God re-creates. God has created man, sin has destroyed him, and God is re-creating and rebuilding man unto Himself. In the re-creative process, He will woo and pursue us with a love that simply will not let us go until the re-creation is done. Let us again look at the Book of Jeremiah and see how God dealt with His people as He established a covenant of deliverance. That is, He promised that those who serve and love Him, He will restore, He will re-create. Read what the Lord said about the condition of His people's hearts:

> This is what the LORD says: "Your wound is incurable, your injury beyond healing. There is no one to plead

your cause, no remedy for your sore, no healing for you. All your allies have forgotten you; they care nothing for you. I have struck you as an enemy would and punished you as would the cruel, because your guilt is so great and your sins so many. Why do you cry out over your wound, your pain that has no cure? Because of your great guilt and many sins I have done these things to you. (Jer. 30:12-15)

This is a picture of a people who had strayed and whose sins were destroying their lives. "Your guilt is so great and your sins so many. Your pain has no cure," said the Lord. How often does our selfishness and poor behavior ruin relationships and harm our future? Often indeed, I'm afraid. So it was with Israel, God's people. All of God's people are similar in that we yearn for a God who can deliver us from both the penalty and power of sin; the penalty because it is one that we cannot pay with anything less than death and eternal separation from God, and power because sin has a way of searing relationships and scarring hearts—making them cold and callous. God, the gracious God, secures deliverance (salvation) from both the penalty (justification) and the power (sanctification) of sin. He is a God who binds and restores that which sin has torn down; He re-creates the heart of His people:

> "But all who devour you will be devoured; all your enemies will go into exile. Those who plunder you will be plundered; all who make spoil of you I will despoil. But I will restore you to health and heal your wounds," declares the LORD. . . . "So you will be my people, and I will be your God." (Jer. 30:16-17, 22)

So we see that God works by creating and by re-creating.
Finally, let us use a much less esoteric example and imagine the life of young Jesus. True, there is little in Scripture that directly speaks about His youth save the account of Jesus being left in Jerusalem during Passover and finally being found in the Temple. We do know, however, that Jesus' formal public ministry did not begin until after he was baptized by John the Baptist at the age of thirty. Only then did He enter the synagogue, where as Jewish custom had it, any commoner could rise up and read from the writings of the Torah or prophets. Jesus, as

Highlight #1

God is a worker and He has created us to be workers.

Time Management Principle #1

View time as a resource to be spent wisely.

prophetic annunciation of the start of His public ministry, read Isaiah:

> The Spirit of the Lord is on me, because he has anointed me to preach good news to the poor. He has sent me to proclaim freedom for the prisoners and recovery of sight for the blind, to release the oppressed, to proclaim year of the Lord's favor. (Luke 4:18-19)

The inference is this: if Jesus began His full-time, formal public ministry at the age of thirty, then He must not have had a full-time, formal public ministry before then. What then did He do? It is reasonable to believe that Jesus did what most Christians do—He worked and ministered simultaneously. That is, He worked six days a week until He was thirty years of age. Let us use our imagination a little and see Jesus, on hands and knees, in well-worn sandals and a sweaty and dirt-laden smock, driving nails, lifting stones, polishing wood, and laying roofing. He worked as a carpenter. There is no biblical evidence that Jesus used this job as a platform for evangelism or that He was piloting an early version of Habitat for Humanity. In fact, there is no biblical evidence that Jesus did anything earth-shattering ministry-wise during His first thirty years of life except that He "grew in wisdom and stature, and in favor with God and men" (Luke 2:52). We assume that He worked and we know that He grew.

It is an interesting thought when one surmises that the Son of God worked for the majority of His life, to imagine Jesus sinking His dry and calloused hands onto the wheelbarrow of work. To work and to glorify His God. To work and to be taught and matured and molded by God. To work and to provide for Himself and His family. It was in those thirty years of working, studying, praying, laughing, loving, and even playing that Jesus became the Man who would ultimately save a people from their sin. Work meant something in the providential plan of our Savior's life and it means something in His plan for ours.

The Need for Time Management

Have you ever set out to accomplish any number of

projects only to look back some time later without any real results and wonder where all the time went? Have you ever said to yourself, "If only I had a couple of extra hours in the day"? Have you ever wondered how some people get so much done in so little time? These feelings are universal; everyone experiences a sense of inadequacy in managing time. This has been a problem since creation. Time simply slips away unless we choose intentionally to use it wisely.

Time management is key if you desire to be a successful premed student and ultimately a successful physician. Perhaps you know enough about the life of a medical student to wonder how you're going to stay ahead of the professor, "review, review, review," or study six to twelve months in advance for the MCAT. Maybe you also have band practice, Bible study, social functions, and family responsibilities, and there is no way you have time for everything. Let me reassure you that with successful time management, you'll be surprised at what you can accomplish. Do not give up hope for excellence until you have tried to manage your time wisely. To do that, understand and follow three principles.

Principles of Time Management

We must begin by understanding that time is a resource. Resources are supplies, either material or nonmaterial, you draw upon to achieve an end. Money is perhaps the most well-known material resource. We use it to purchase goods necessary for living. We have a finite amount; when it's gone, it's gone. Time is, fundamentally speaking, the same. It is a resource just as money is a resource; we spend our time and then it's gone. We may spend it wisely or we may spend it foolishly. Either way, our life and time here are short. The prophet Isaiah lamented it in this way:

> All men are like grass, and all their glory is like the flowers of the field. The grass withers and the flowers fall, because the breath of the LORD blows on them. Surely the people are grass. (Isa. 40:6-7)

Moses also knew the reality of life's brevity when he said,

> The length of our days is seventy years—or eighty, if we have the strength; yet their span is but trouble and

sorrow, for they quickly pass, and we fly away. (Ps. 90:10)

Time is a nonmaterial resource that is in limited supply.

Let us understand here that all resources, though limited, are given to us by God. Money, time, energy, relationships, and talent—He has given us all of these supplies necessary for life. Since He is the giver of all things, these resources are not ours but His. He has given them to us to use for His purposes. We are stewards or managers of these resources. We are managers for the King! And we are accountable to Him for how we spend everything we've received. Jesus described our responsibility in this parable:

A man of noble birth went to a distant country to have himself appointed king and then to return. So he called ten of his servants and gave them ten minas. "Put this money to work," he said, "until I come back." But his subjects hated him and sent a delegation after him to say, "We don't want this man to be our king." He was made king, however, and returned home. Then he sent for the servants to whom he had given the money, in order to find out what they had gained with it. The first one came and said, "Sir, your mina has earned ten more." "Well done, my good servant!" his master replied. "Because you have been trustworthy in a very small matter, take charge of ten cities." The second came and said, "Sir, your mina has earned five more." His master answered, "You take charge of five cities." Then another servant came and said, "Sir, here is your mina; I have kept it laid away in a piece of cloth. I was afraid of you, because you are a hard man. You take out what you did not put in and reap what you did not sow." His master replied, "I will judge you by your own words, you wicked servant! You knew, did you, that I am a hard man, taking out what I did not put in, and reaping what I did not sow? Why then didn't you put my money on deposit, so that when I came back, I could have collected it with interest?" Then he said to those standing by, "Take his mina away from him and give it to the one who has ten minas." "Sir," they said, "he already has ten!" He replied, "I tell you that to everyone who has, more will

Highlight #2

Time is a resource given by God; we are to be responsible with it.

be given, but as for the one who has nothing, even what he has will be taken away." (Luke 19:12-26)

According to the parable, the roles are clear. Jesus is the master, and we are His servants. He has given us resources and commanded us to invest them. Understand that Jesus is not principally interested in our IRS statements or our Day-timers; He is interested in our hearts! He wants us to invest every resource He has given us for His glory. This means that we can't do just anything we wish with our money and time.

It's important to realize, as the parable illustrates, that how you manage your resources—money, time, energy, relationships, and talents—is a reflection of your heart. What you invest in is a consequence of where your heart is. For instance, if my greatest and only ambition in life were to play professional basketball, then that would be what all of my thoughts, dreams, and actions revolved around. I would invest all of my resources toward that goal: which college I attended, how I spent my free time, why I studied (to maintain a GPA that enabled me to play on the college team), what I spent my money on ($200 basketball sneakers and $200 warm-ups, plus a real leather basketball). You get the picture: I would manage my resources as a reflection of where my heart was.

The principle here is this: time is a limited resource given us by God, and we are to be wise stewards of it. As stewards, we must both manage our hearts wisely by investing them in valuable things and manage our resources wisely as they will reflect where our hearts are. We must, as Peter exhorted, "use whatever gift [we have] received to serve others, faithfully administering God's grace in its various forms" (1 Peter 4:10).

The second principle we need to understand has to do with determining where we spend the resource of time. Charles Hummel wrote this about priorities:

> We live in constant tension between the urgent and the important. The problem is that many important tasks need not be done today or even this week. . . . But often the urgent, though less important, tasks call for immediate response—endless demands pressure every waking hour. . . . The appeal of these demands seems irresistible, and they devour our energy. But in

Time Management Principle #2
Discern between what is urgent and what is important.

the light of eternity their momentary prominence fades. With a sense of loss we recall the important tasks that have been shunted aside. We realize that we've become slaves to the tyranny of the urgent.[1]

Hummel said that we have pushed aside things that are really important in life for things that are not but that simply demand our attention in a stronger manner. In the process we have become slaves to these unimportant tasks and in doing so are weary and joyless.

Highlight #3

Ask God to help you be a better steward of the resource of time.

A good friend of mine, who also happens to be an otolaryngology resident, once taught me an exercise to help decide what in life is urgent and what is important. As a surgical subspecialty resident he found it exceedingly important that his own time was well-managed, so he found this exercise helpful and meaningful. Obviously, this is a dynamic exercise, always changing, as things that are important to you now may or may not be as you grow older. Also, things that are perhaps not so urgent in your life now may become more urgent later. Nevertheless, this method is a wonderful tool to illustrate the second principle of time management: discern between the urgent and the important things in your life.

First, take a moment and ask God to show you what the important things in your life are versus what things are urgent. Ask God to help you "live—not as unwise but as wise, making the most of every opportunity" (Eph. 5:15-16). Ask God to help you be a better steward of the resource of time.

Next, take a sheet of paper and with a pencil, divide it into four squares. Label it like the diagram below.

To the best of your ability, categorize every activity you do during the day. Keep in mind that important things are truly significant and meaning-

	Urgent	Not Urgent
Not Important		
Important		

ful; urgent things demand your immediate attention but may not be as important. Everything should fit into one of these four categories. For instance, you might put laundry into the Not Important but Urgent category (although for some of my bachelor friends, I would say it is important and urgent!). Watching television might be not important and not urgent. Writing a belated letter to your dear friend may fit into the Important but Not Urgent category. Cleaning up your apartment may be urgent because you're tripping over things, but a better use of your time would be spending some extra hours studying for that upcoming exam—it's just more important.

As you work on this exercise, recognize that there are no right or wrong answers, for in truth, some things are important to me that are simply not important for you and vice versa. Be honest with yourself. If you are not sure what is important, go to the Scriptures. God will show you through His Word:

Time Management Principle #3
Organize and budget your time.

> All Scripture is God-breathed and is useful for teaching, rebuking, correcting and training in righteousness, so that the man of God may be thoroughly equipped for every good work. (2 Tim. 3:16)

The Book of Proverbs, especially, reveals what God considers of highest priority.

After you have determined what is important versus what is urgent, try to begin doing the important ones—the truly meaningful things—more than the urgent. Do the urgent things as actually necessary, but let the important things take precedence. This may mean setting limits on how much television you can watch or perhaps purchasing an answering machine so you can spend more uninterrupted time studying. It will not be easy. You will have to refer often to this chart and make disciplined decisions based on it. It will take a tremendous level of spiritual and emotional maturity to say no to the urgent in light of the important; purpose that through God's grace you will act not as a child but as a man or woman. God will grow and mature you.

> When I was a child, I talked like a child, I thought like a child, I reasoned like a child. When I became a man, I put childish ways behind me. (1 Cor. 13:11)

God will help you begin to replace the urgent things with the important things in life. Naturally, then, what is urgent and what is important will change over time. Periodically rework this exercise to keep up with the shifting demands in your life.

The third principle involves organization. Now that you understand that time is a resource just like any other resource, it must not be wasted, and that it must be spent on the important instead of the urgent as much as possible, you can now organize and budget your time. When I was in college, I worked in a laboratory under a student work scholarship and drew a modest stipend. For most of my years in college I lived at home, so since I did not have any monthly bills to pay, this money should have been accumulating. However, to my surprise, I never seemed to save a dime! It just went in one hand and out the other. I decided that for one week, I was going to take an inventory of where my money was going. I thought surely I could not be spending it all on measly candy bars and a CD here and there. I recorded every penny that I spent for that week, every meal eaten out, every paperback purchased, every date I went on (a fictitious example!). It turned out that 80 percent of my weekly paycheck was going toward fast food. It did not take me long to figure out that I needed to keep my snacking at a minimum if I was going to save any money.

I would suggest the same approach to you: inventory your time.

Monday, 9/23

Time	Activity	Time	Activity
6:45	brushed, showered	3:15	browsed through music store
7:15	ate breakfast	4:00	did math homework
7:45	walked to class	5:00	called Christy
9:00	class	6:00	dinner
9:50	walked to student union	6:30	watch TV
10:00	browsed through bookstore	7:00	shot hoops with the guys
10:30	played football	8:30	read chapter for English quiz
11:00	class	9:30	answered email messages
12:00	went to dorm room, listened to music	10:00	met Christy at coffee house
12:30	lunch	11:45	went back to dorm
1:00	class		
2:00	played ping pong with Ross		

Inventory

hygiene: 0:30
eating: 1:30
transportation: 0:50
class: 3:40

study: 2:00
downtime/recreation: 4:30
social: 4:00

Record every minute spent for an entire week, or even for just an entire day. Carry around a small pad of paper and a pen and record what you do, noting the time at which you transition from one activity to the next. Include watching TV, talking on the phone, studying, eating, sleeping, and so on.

You may think this is useless, you know how you spend your time, and there simply isn't anymore. But my hunch is that you will find that you are spending entirely too much time doing things that fall into the Urgent but Not Important or the Not

				1	2	3
4	5	6	7	8	9 small group	10
11	12	13	14	15 Biology test	16 small group	17
18	19 Math test	20	21	22	23 small group	24
25	26	27	28 history paper	29	30 ---------out of	31 town---------

Urgent and Not Important categories. A sample inventory may look like the list to the left.

Next, purchase monthly, weekly, and daily calendars. You can typically find these at any office supply store or through national mail order companies. The use of a monthly calender lets you see the big picture, a significant chunk of time and the major events during that time. On this monthly calender put events such as tests, term-paper deadlines, any foreseen absences, retreats, dates, etc. This will give you a general feel for how much time you will have between major events. A sample monthly calender might look like the schedule on this page.

Your weekly calender comes next. Let's assume that at the end of the week you will have a biology test and at the start of the following week you will have a math test. Your weekly calender then is a day-by-day breakdown of roughly five or six things that need to be accomplished to prepare you for those major events. For instance, on

Monday you may choose to:
- Read chapter 2 in your biology book.
- Listen to the tape of that lecture.
- Go over those notes another time.
- Work math problems 1-35 in chapter 5.
- Work math problems 1-20 in chapter 6.

On Tuesday you may choose to:
- Read chapter 3 in your biology book.
- Listen to the tape of that lecture.
- Go over those notes another time.
- Attend the review session for the biology test.

MONDAY

1. Outline Ch 2 of Biology book
2. Listen to tape on that lecture
3. Review notes
4. Problems 1-35, Ch 2 in Math
5. Problems 1-29, Ch 3 in Math
6. Review Chemistry and Speech notes

TUESDAY

1. Outline Ch 3 of Biology book
2. Listen to tape on that lecture
3. Review those notes
4. Go to review session
5. Review Chemistry and Speech notes

WEDNESDAY

1. Read first 40 pages of History assignment
2. Outline Ch 4 of Biology book
3. Problems 1-25-odd in Chemistry Ch 4
4. Go to Chemistry study group
5. Review Chemistry and Speech notes

THURSDAY

1. Problems 26-44--even in Chemistry CH 4
2. Review all notes
3. Catch up on all work that is behind

FRIDAY

1. Listen to tape on Ch 4 Biology lecture and take notes
2. Work of speech outline
3. Review all notes

SATURDAY/SUNDAY

1. Problems 1-30--odd in Chemistry CH 5
2. Outline Ch 5 Biology book
3. Listen to tape of that lecture
4. Problems 1-33 Ch 4 in Math
5. Go to Library to research speech
6. Review all notes

You are probably getting the idea. I need to mention that it may be helpful to schedule two weeks at a time because not every major event is broken up so neatly into weekly slots. Make sure that you schedule slots to make up for the possibility of falling behind. In other words, you may choose to list "make-up time" as one of your choices. Use it to catch up on anything that you weren't able to do in the previous days. I would advise against scheduling study slots right up to the time of the test day. What usually happens is that you fall behind and you end up studying half of the material extremely well, and then half of the material in a huge rush! Schedule to finish studying a day or two before the test. That way, if you do fall behind, you will have a couple of days to catch up. If not, it will be time to review or even relax before a test (it could happen!). A sample weekly schedule might look like the calendar on this page.

The final step is to make out daily schedules. This can be done at the beginning of the week or the night previous. This schedule is one that outlines your entire day from 6 A.M. to 12 A.M. Include when to sleep, when to eat, when and what your classes are, from what time to what time you will study and which subjects, study breaks, free time, etc. Do not neglect scheduling breaks and free time or you will quickly find this method to be impractical. Allot yourself a little more time than you think you need so you will not rush through important things. Let me encourage you to schedule in plenty of sleep. If you stay on track, you will not only need it, you will deserve it. A sample daily calendar might look like the schedule to the right.

How to Press On

I confess that time management is not easy. It is not something that comes naturally to most people, least of all me. I had little success in the beginning. I would schedule and not stick to it or I would schedule and then stop scheduling. It became obvious I did not possess a consistent commitment to manage time wisely. Finally, realizing that I did not have the strength to make scheduling work, I did what I should have done in the first place: I asked God to be Lord of my time.

God answered, but not in the way I thought He would. I thought He would make me more strong-willed, more physically fit, more clever in time management skills. In fact, He did none of these. He did, however, give me something that provided me the strength and the will to be disciplined in my time management: He gave me vision.

Vision is merely clear-sightedness. It is vision that allows us to see spiritual death all around us; it is vision that allows us to see God's infinite grace at the cross; it is vision that allows us to see our need of it. God also gives us a vision for our lives. He allows us to see, as clearly as if it were reality, where He wants us and why. It is not a dream or a hallucination, but the confidence of heart that has heard God say, "Wherever you are, I am with you." It says that He has gifted us uniquely and that He will use those gifts for His glory and our good.

There is a tremendous release and freedom in seeing and believing that God has a plan for our lives. Vision, not time management, empowers. Ask God for vision to see

Monday, March 5	
6 am	
7 am	Get up, shower, quiet time, breakfast
8 am	Chemistry 1201 lecture
9 am	Biology 1001 lecture
10 am	30 minute break, pay bills
11 am	Speech lecture
12 pm	Lunch, 15 minute break
1 pm	Outline half of Ch 2 Biology book
2 pm	Listen to Biology Ch 2 tape
3 pm	Snack, 20 minute break
4 pm	Outline other half of Ch 2 Biology book
5 pm	Go to rec center to exercise
6 pm	Dinner with guys
7 pm	Problems 11-35 Math Ch 2, 1-10 Ch 3
8 pm	(continued)
9 pm	15 minute break
10 pm	Review biology notes
11 pm	Wind down, sleep
12 am	

Highlight #4

Vision, not time management, empowers.

people's need of grace and vision to see and believe that God has a specific plan for your life. If you believe this, you will not have to muster up your greatest effort only to see it fail four or five days later. You will walk peacefully at what others may deem a rapid pace. Ask God for vision in your life.

Points to Ponder

1. Have you ever pictured God as a worker who enjoys His work? If not, how have you seen Him?

2. What does Jesus' working for thirty years before beginning His three-year ministry mean to you?

3. How have you managed your time till now? What tools or methods have worked? Which haven't?

4. Take time to make an urgent/important chart. Share with the group items that are clearly one or the other, then talk about what items are hard to label.

5. Why is vision so necessary?

Notes

1. Charles E. Hummel, *Tyranny of the Urgent* (Downers Grove, IL: InterVarsity Press, 1967), 5-6.

Part II
The Work

Chapter 4
Grades, MCAT,
and Letters of
Recommendation

All things excellent are as difficult as they are rare.
—Benedict Spinoza

All hard work brings a profit, but mere talk leads only to poverty.
—Proverbs 14:23

Now that we have discussed general principles regarding the mindset of a Christian premedical student, let us discuss the specifics of this work—the nuts and bolts of premed. Your work during the first three years of college culminates in a very important document: your medical school application. There is a temptation at times to look rather cynically at the process of medical school application. Sometimes it appears to be reduced to a game that must be played. Admittedly, the process can get fatiguing.

But be encouraged! Trust that the physicians on the admission committees know what they are doing. After all, they have been through both college and medical school. They know that the discipline of preparing all week for an organic chemistry exam when the rest of your friends are playing basketball will show when several years down the road you study all week for a pathology exam when the rest of the world is watching the Final Four on TV.

All aspects of your application are important and need to be addressed because they can and will be useful somewhere in your medical training. There are three major components in an application that admissions committee members look at. First and foremost is *academic achievement.* This includes grades, MCAT, letters of recommendation, honors, and awards. The committee wants to see if the applicant can handle the intellectual rigors of medical school. Are you smart?

Second is *exposure to the field.* This includes hospital volunteer work and research experience. The committee wants to see if the applicant is really interested in medicine. Are you eager?

Third is *personal qualities.* This includes activities during college, letters of recommendation, a personal statement about your goals, and interviews. The committee wants to see if the applicant is someone whose personality fits medicine. Are you humane?

We will explore the first component in this chapter.

Grades

Never underestimate the power of good grades. They show that the applicant is intellectual, hardworking, and stable—

perhaps the most important qualities an admissions committee looks for. Grades do not tell everything about an applicant, but nevertheless, they are probably still the most important part of an application.

In fact, it has been my experience that one cannot overcome poor grades with any other component of the application and be admitted into medical school. However, one can overcome a weakness in any other component of the application *with* good grades. Although simplified and therefore not always true, here is a way of expressing the importance of grades.

Great Grades + Mediocre Remainder = Admission
but
Mediocre Grades + Great Remainder = *Possible* Admission

There are exceptions to this rule. A friend of mine earned a 2.5 GPA his first year in college. He subsequently improved his grades and graduated with a 3.2 GPA, but made 4.0's in both of his last two semesters. The local medical school where he applied had applicants with higher grade point averages than his 3.2, but the administrators saw his overall progression and during his interview were impressed with his maturity, and decided to admit him. Realize, however, that this is by far the exception. For every similar success story there are probably ten who did not get accepted solely because of mediocre grades. Great grades mean a lot.

Most medical schools will never admit to a formula, but it is a well-known fact that one's grades, first, and MCAT scores, second, convey the basic, overall admissions picture. This picture is of paramount importance to making the first cut. For instance, if University Medical School X receives three thousand applications this year, it may decide to interview eight hundred candidates. To determine who gets an interview, there will likely be a grid where GPAs and MCAT scores are plotted two-dimensionally. There will be an arbitrary cutoff and those students above the cutoff will receive an interview and those below will not—regardless of extracurricular activities, research, leadership, or letters of recommendation. These qualifications have bearing only in the second cut, that is, deciding which of the eight hundred interviewed will be offered a

Most medical schools will never admit to a formula, but it is a well-known fact that one's grades, first, and MCAT scores, second, convey the basic overall admissions picture.

spot. Therefore, bad scores mean no interview, and no interview means no admission.

Tips for Better Grades

Highlight #1

Great Grades + Mediocre Remainder = Admission but Mediocre Grades + Great Remainder = Possible Admission

1. Take a light course load.

I have a friend who never took more than fourteen hours a semester. She had the option of going to summer school and the ability to skip a number of college classes right out of high school through advanced-placement exams. Having a light course load alone, she says, allowed her to maintain a 4.0 throughout her college career. In addition to the relatively low number of hours, she took fairly easy but nevertheless interesting electives whenever possible to balance her more difficult required science courses. That way, she took only two or three very difficult classes while taking another two or three easy ones. Her general rule of thumb was "Only two big guns per semester!" Before you deem this too light of a load, read my other suggestions. Afterward you may think otherwise. Remember, "Much study wearies the body" (Eccl. 12:12). Minimize the course load to minimize the weariness! You will need the energy to pursue excellence.

2. Be willing to commit overkill.

Learn to study and purpose to know everything possible about the topic you're being tested on. Never assume "the professor will never ask that"—it always manages to show up on the test the minute you say that. Do not be lazy and cut corners. Study beyond what you may think is necessary. Scripture tells us "Diligent hands will rule, but laziness forfeits any reward" (Prov. 12:24). Shoot for the moon—you just may make it over the barn.

3. Stay ahead of, not even with, your professors.

It is advisable to stay one or two chapters ahead of the professor. Then lectures will be review instead of new material. The problem with hearing a topic for the first time in class is that if you become confused at any point, the rest of the lecture may be useless. You will just rush to copy everything from the chalkboard into your notebook with the intention of figuring it out at home. How much more profitable it is if the lecture simply becomes an exercise of reaffirmation and clarification of previously studied information! This means that one should talk with the professor before the class starts, get a syllabus, and start studying a week or two before the semester starts to get ahead—then purpose to study each night to stay ahead. Borrowing from Proverbs again:

> Four things on earth are small, yet they are extremely wise: ants are creatures of little strength, yet they store up their food in the summer. (Prov. 30:24-25)

It is extremely wise to prepare in advance. Get ahead and stay ahead.

4. Become an expert note-taker.

Your notes are only as useful to you before a test as they are full of good information. Here are several lines of advice related to note-taking:

Sit in the front row. I realize this sounds "geekish," but the reality of the situation is that there are more distractions the farther back you sit. In the front row, there is nothing to look at—or concentrate on—except a black-board and a professor. (This is also helpful in building a relationship with your professor—something important if you later need a letter of recommendation or if your grade is on the borderline.)

Minimize your course load to minimize the weariness.

Write down everything important. This should go without saying, but all too often I have seen that students just do not write that much. Their notes end up as rough outlines of the lecture, or contain only a few phrases or sentences. You may not be able to write everything down, but write down all that you can. Go back after class and verify with the professor what you missed.

Tape-record important and difficult classes. If a class has the reputation of being difficult or if it is a vitally important one, tape and listen to it immediately following class. Addend your notes during this time to make sure you have everything written down.

Make an outline of your notes. At some time before your test, distill your notes by making notes of them. This seems tedious and a waste of time, but you will be surprised how much better you retain the material by doing this. You are essentially reinforcing the lessons by teaching them to yourself and then taking notes on your own mental lessons. You are acting on the proverb "See one, do one, teach one" by reteaching yourself the lesson and then rewriting it down.

Use mnemonics. Mnemonics are devices used to enhance recall and memory. For example, the three most common mediastinal masses are "the three T's": thymomas, teratomas, and terrible lymphomas. You probably learned a mnemonic in high school for the colors of the rainbow: ROY-G-BIV (red, orange, yellow, green, blue, indigo, and violet). You can even make up a story and draw it if it helps you to get the order of nerves or blood vessels right for an anatomy test. The more creative, the easier to remember. Use mnemonics in your notes.

Review. God instructed His servant Joshua to constantly review in his mind the early Scriptures (Josh. 1:8). We are creatures who tend to easily forget spiritual lessons. So much more so it is with the more mundane topics of life such as glycolysis and hydrogen bonding. Therefore, it is advisable to review for twenty to thirty minutes the information taught in class within the first twenty-four hours after you hear it. This way the information is fresh and can be reinforced easily. It is not advisable to wait until the week of the exam to rehash material taught weeks ago, because the information that *was* there, if not immediately processed, was quickly discarded. Therefore, review immediately.

5. Don't miss class.

I did not skip a class until the last semester of my senior year when I decided that I should try it and see what all the hoopla was about. So, instead of going into my 11:30 biochemistry class, I simply sat outside the doors for an hour. I must say, skipping class is really overrated! Seriously, one of the greatest temptations in college is skipping class because unlike in high school—you can! However, missing class works only to your own detriment. You pick up more in class than you think. Even if you felt you did not understand the material, at least you have been introduced to it. There will be nuances pertaining to the topics at hand that you pick up just by listening to the professor—you won't have those if you study the material straight out of the book. Also, professors will hint at test questions, placing emphasis on specific topics, while downplaying others. Some may even come right out and say what will or will not

Start studying a week or two before the semester starts to get ahead.

be on the test. Try to avoid oversleeping—show up, even at that 7:30 A.M. class! (If you think 7:30 is early, remember that as a medical student, you may begin the day at 4:30!) I love the brutal honesty of Solomon when he said,

> Do not love sleep or you will grow poor; stay awake and you will have food to spare. (Prov. 20:13)

6. Don't cram.

There is a tendency to wait until three days before the test, panic, study all night, and cram right up to the test. Pulling all-nighters is not something I recommend. In fact, cramming does not work. The brain can only process so much information so fast. It needs time to "digest"—days and weeks, not minutes and hours. In fact, so much information is processed while we sleep that by not sleeping, we actually deprive ourselves of efficient learning. If you work diligently and in an organized fashion, you will not have to cram.

7. Get to know your professors.

Ask your professors questions during and after class. Show up in their offices during office hours and politely ask more questions! I would even suggest making up hypothetical questions if for nothing else than to introduce yourself and to maintain a habit of getting to know your professors. This serves two purposes: informational and personal. In your session, you will unexpectedly pick up gems that are important concepts to understand—gems that often show up on tests. Also, you will be paving a road that you may return on one day to ask for a recommendation letter.

8. Learn to say No.

There are many, many opportunities to be a part of truly worthwhile events during college. Have the maturity to say "Not now" if you know that you have more important ways to spend your time. To paraphrase the Ecclesiastical preacher, "There is a time to play and a time to work." College, it must be said, is a time to work. In fact, I believe that the first two years of college may be the most strategic and have the highest investment potential in one's life! This is why: if one does exceedingly well in one's freshman and sophomore classes, it can generally be said that one will

Highlight #2
The first two years of college may be the most strategic and have the highest investment potential in one's life!

71

Tips for Better Grades

1. Take a light course load.

2. Be willing to commit overkill.

3. Stay ahead of, not even with, your professors.

4. Become an expert note-taker.

5. Don't miss class.

6. Don't cram.

7. Get to know your professors.

8. Learn to say No.

also do well in junior-level classes, because often junior-level classes contain much overlap. For example, much of microbial genetics was simply microbiology, biology, and genetics. If I learned the basics well the first time, then the new material was easy to learn. However, if I did not take the time to learn them well in my first two years, the new material was exceedingly difficult.

Furthermore, it is only these three years that count toward your grade point average when you apply to medical school. Admissions personnel will not, by and large, see your senior-level grades. If these grades, then, are good and you are accepted into a reputable medical school, you can study while in medical school with full assurance that your future as a physician is relatively secure. At that point, the work is voluminous but the pressure is off. Your investment in the first two years of college has paid huge dividends. It has secured, indirectly, your field of work.

Two friends come to mind to as examples. The first one was a friend from high school who was very popular—I'll call her Stephanie. Stephanie was student body president, prom queen, and teacher's pet. In terms of popularity, she had it all together. However, when she went to college, Stephanie dropped out of sight for two years. For all of her previous social success, she sure took a nose-dive! In fact, she simply locked herself in a library and became exactly what everyone thought she was not—a serious student. In time, she resurfaced and became president of three organizations, worked with the dean of the college, and published a research paper—but not until her junior year when her grades were already entirely secure. She was ultimately accepted into Harvard Medical School and is enjoying herself and her life as of last report.

My second friend, "Jake," decided that college would be a lot of fun. In all fairness, it was difficult for him because it was the first time Jake had lived away from home and that external discipline was suddenly gone. Consequently Jake played basketball until the recreation center closed every night. He went out with friends on the weekend to church and school functions. When tests came around, he crammed all night. Jake finished college with a 2.7 GPA and has worked the last four years of his life in a research lab, taking graduate courses and reapplying to medical schools all over the country. He says with remorse that he is paying for his "fun" now.

If you can get into medical school, you can get through medical school. The key is getting in, and the key to getting in is diligent work in the first two years of college. Invest the first two years of college into your grades. Learn to say No to other things.

The Medical College Admission Test (MCAT)

The Medical College Admission Test is a 345-minute, 219-question, and two-essay test broken up into four parts: verbal reasoning, physical sciences, biological sciences, and writing. The verbal reasoning section measures comprehension, analysis, and integration of general information. The two science sections synthesize basic biology, inorganic chemistry, organic chemistry, and physics and measures basic concepts and the application of such information. The writing section assesses one's skills in presenting themes clearly, logically, and intelligently.

Highlight #3
Know that different medical schools will place different emphasis on MCAT scores.

Know that different medical schools will place different emphasis on MCAT scores. Although the test is required by most medical schools, MCAT scores are not always useful. This test has a history of having little predictive value of success as a medical student, resident, and attending physician. In fact, the medical school I attended no longer requires its applicants to take the MCAT. As a case in point, my medical school roommate was a history major who chose not to take the MCAT. Not only did the school admit him, it funded his entire medical school education!

However, sometimes MCAT scores are particularly valuable. If the applicant is from a little-known undergraduate program, a competitive MCAT score is an equalizer. It is a standard for comparison between institutions of varied repute. Also, some medical schools will accept a certain number of applicants based solely on their grade point averages and MCAT scores if they are high enough.

Tips for Better MCAT Performance

1. Prepare from day one.
In other words, learn the material well from your classes.

Tips for the MCAT

1. Prepare from day one.

2. Study six to twelve months in advance.

3. Use all available resources.

The best way to do well on genetics questions on the MCAT is to have learned it well when it was taught in class! This way studying for the MCAT will be an exercise of recall (which is far more efficient) rather than an exercise of learning new information. At least half of how well you do on test day is determined by how well you have done in the three years previous to that day. The top ten MCAT scores at my undergraduate institution were made by the top students grade-wise.

To illustrate this point, let me point to one occurrence in the life of British Prime Minister Benjamin Disraeli. One day, in the House of Commons, he made a brilliant speech on the spur of the moment. That night a friend said to him, "'I must tell you how much I enjoyed your extemporaneous talk. It's been on my mind all day." "Madam," confessed Disraeli, "that extemporaneous talk has been on my mind for twenty years!"[1] Disraeli performed brilliantly in his short talk because in truth he had been preparing for twenty years—stewing, mulling over thoughts, articulating. The same can be said for MCAT preparation. Brilliance is not achieved overnight. The six hours of testing will not, in large part, be a reflection of the six days or weeks or even six months of preparation beforehand, but the three long years of college that culminate in a relatively short six-hour exam. Prepare for the MCAT by performing well in your classes.

2. Study six to twelve months in advance.

Although much is based on your previous years' study, it is possible to study for this exam. It does not matter if you do it through an $800 course or a $40 book. Just study at least six months before you take the test. You can find good guidelines in *A Complete Preparation for the MCAT: The Betz Guide* and *Flowers and Silver MCAT Preparation*. It is advisable to downsize your course load the semester of the MCAT so you're able to set aside time specifically for MCAT study.

3. Use all available resources.

You can order a copy of *The MCAT Student Manual* and *The Practice Medical College Admission Test*. These resources contain helpful questions from the MCAT as well as the types of questions and subjects to be covered.

Order these from The Association of American Medical Colleges, Attn: Membership and Publication Orders, 2450 N Street N.W., Washington, DC 20037-1129.

Letters of Recommendation

King Solomon said that "a good name is more desirable than great riches" (Prov. 22:1). Letters of recommendation are opportunities for you to let admissions committee members know your "good name"—the kind of person you are as well as the accomplishments you have achieved. Admissions committees will want to know that you have maturity, dedication, intelligence, stability, a strong work ethic, organization, and leadership ability. The letters provide the committee members with windows into your life in a way that your grades and MCAT scores cannot. The letters alone will not get you into medical school, but they can make the difference between being at the top or the bottom of a stack of qualified applicants.

Highlight #4

A letter from a "nobody" that is colorful, detailed, and persuasive is far stronger than a bland one from someone "famous."

Tips for Better Letters of Recommendation

1. Prepare from day one.
Jesus Himself prepared for thirty years before officially beginning His three short years of ministry. The principle of preparedness cannot be overemphasized. Just as it is profitable to prepare in advance for classes and the MCAT, so it is with letters of recommendation. You may not as a freshman already know all of your professors, but start thinking ahead and tentatively plan on asking any number of professors. That way you will be prepared to make good impressions on them when you take their classes. Again, get to know these professors during the classes so they can write something good about you.

2. Choose people who know you.
This seems obvious but there are many people who seek letters from deans, chairmen, or even Nobel Laureates— letters from acquaintances yield only generic comments about the individual. A letter from a "nobody" that is colorful, detailed, and persuasive is far stronger than a bland

Tips for Letters of Recommendation

1. Prepare from day one.

2. Choose people who know you.

3. Get letters from a variety of professors.

4. Prepare a portfolio.

one from someone "famous." Good letters of recommendation indicate that you have demonstrated the potential to be an excellent physician, academically and spiritually, and someone has noticed.

3. Get letters from a variety of professors.

Do not get five letters from chemistry professors, which all say the same thing. If, for example, you want five letters (which may not be necessary), ask professors of philosophy, music, and biochemistry as well as a couple of chemistry instructors. This will show that you are well-rounded. Not every professor will know all aspects of your character. That is why it is important to select evaluators who can cover qualities that other evaluators cannot. However, in your effort to maintain diversity, recognize that your evaluators should be college faculty and not pastors or family members. The latter, unfortunately, carry little or no weight.

4. Prepare a portfolio.

Let me emphasize something: professors want to write a good recommendation letter for you. So help them! Give them a folder with your picture, a list of your grades, honors/awards, and extracurricular activities. Even write out personal statements about yourself. I was approached by a professor who had been asked by a student to write a letter on his behalf. This professor was kind and agreed to write it but did not really know this student well. He did know, however, that this student and I were good friends and so he asked me about the student's qualities! Let me repeat: professors want to see you succeed and want to write a good letter for you. Help by giving them all the resources possible.

The Work Accomplished . . . Almost

What a sense of relief and accomplishment when at the end of your third year or at the beginning of your fourth year of premed your committee and counselors mail to the medical schools of your choice your compiled grades, MCAT scores, and letters of recommendation! You have worked long and hard to show medical schools that you have the academic capabilities to become a physician and you deserve a pat on the back.

However, you also know that it is not just the academic side of you that is impressive to admissions committees, but also the personal side of you. You know that the medical schools will see not only an intelligent young man or woman, but also one who has had enough experience in the field to know that medicine is the right choice of careers. They will see that you are an honest, caring, committed applicant and that you will make a very good doctor on an emotional level. You know these things because you have prepared in advance and have proactively sought out opportunities to show admissions committees these qualities of yours.

It is this process we will discuss next.

Points to Ponder

1. Which of the tips for better grades do you routinely follow on your own? Have you found it helpful?

2. What new idea do you need to incorporate in your study habits?

3. Can you think of other methods you could use that might help you become a better student?

4. What have you found particularly difficult to say "no" to that you know is important for you to exclude from your commitments?

5. Who can you add to your study team that will help you stay on track?

Notes

1. Miles Stanford, *The Green Letters: Principles of Spiritual Growth* (Grand Rapids, MI: Zondervan Publishers, 1975), 17.

Chapter 5
Experience and Personal Qualities

When I was a boy of fourteen, my father was so ignorant I could hardly stand to have the old man around. But when I got to be twenty-one, I was astonished at how much the old man had learned in seven years.
—Mark Twain

Every man has three characters—that which he exhibits, that which he has, and that which he thinks he has.
—Alphonse Karr

I
t is true that while grades and MCAT scores are the preliminary and primary credentials medical schools evaluate, experience and personal qualities become more important as the process continues. Upon deciding who has the intellectual capabilities to succeed in medical school and thereby selecting the first tier of students, admissions committees will then turn to *what kind of people* they want to admit.

Experience and personal qualities paint a picture of you, the applicant. They communicate what you are interested in and what you spend your extra time doing. What people do with their free time says a lot. Do they invest the time by participating in activities that will pay dividends later—activities that build character, vision, wisdom, and health? Or do they waste the time in fruitless pursuits? Paul encouraged the church at Ephesus to live wisely, "making the most of every opportunity, because the days are evil" (Eph. 5:13). Time is perhaps a physician's most precious commodity, and to show that one can manage it and commit to meaningful experiences speaks volumes about the applicant's maturity.

Let me encourage you to choose just one, at most two, primary extracurricular activities at a time. I am not denying that humans need to recreate, but I know from experience that it must be done in moderation in order to keep academics a priority. I have always believed that college is a place where one can choose to be great at one thing and one thing only, good at two or three things, or simply average in a number of things. Most college students end up being simply average in a number of things (but they have a tremendous amount of fun in doing so!). Don't let this be your goal. If you feel God has called you into medicine, that must be your focus for now.

It is a valid option to simply not be involved in extracurricular activities during your freshman and sophomore years so you can commit more time to studies. You may then choose during your junior and senior years to become more involved. This is an entirely acceptable approach. Purpose to obtain academic excellence first, and then, having achieved that, commit to some extracurricular activities. When I started college my goal for my freshman and sophomore years was a 4.0 GPA while I was involved with a small Bible study group for accountability and encouragement. It was not until my junior and senior years that I became more involved with leadership organizations, social functions, hospital experience, and research.

Finally, while choosing which of these meaningful activities to participate in, ask yourself how each would shape God's vision for your life. Extracurricular activities are not just hoops that medical schools make you jump through—they are real experiences that should mold your way of thinking and believing. How, you may ask, do these experiences relate to your choosing medicine, or what you think a good doctor is, or what kind of role you will play as a doctor? Remember that ultimately these experiences are for your own personal benefit—not just to impress the medical school. Let God use these experiences to create a vision for your life. Dare to dream big.

> In his heart a man plans his course, but the LORD determines his steps. (Prov. 16:9)

Give yourself the freedom to dream big dreams that God can use and remember that He will direct, shape, and if necessary, remold those dreams.

Highlight #1

Limit extracurricular activities, at least initially.

Hospital Experience

The average physician trains anywhere from seven to fourteen years after graduating college. This is a lot of time to commit; admissions committees want to see that you understand what the field is about and that you are ready to make that commitment. Therefore, they place a premium on experience within a hospital, a clinic, or with a physician. Considering the growing pool of medical-school applicants, this experience is almost a must. It gives the applicant a practical, working knowledge of the medical field and its related specialties, and it also helps the applicant understand the work world, how it is organized, and how it is maintained. The applicant can then imagine himself or herself in the role of physician and better clarify career choices and objectives. It is a strong part of the application that all committees look at.

This experience does not have to be in candy striping, although there is nothing wrong with that. It can be in any form—just have some experience. Here are suggestions on how to get some.

Ways to Get Hospital Experience

1. Volunteer at a hospital.

Most hospitals love volunteers. They recognize that you have little or no medical expertise, but will gladly accept you as you are. Understand, though, that because of this lack of expertise, you typically will not see or do very much for a long time. The best place to find some experience is at a charity hospital where staffing is minimal and rules are generally more relaxed. You could score big if you find a willing resident to tag around with!

2. Volunteer at a nursing home.

Nursing homes are often looking for helping hands and smiling faces. Some nursing homes are so understaffed that they will not balk at asking you to help immediately. In this setting, you can develop your communication skills with older people and become familiar with the physical and spiritual issues of geriatric care.

3. Spend time with a private physician.

Ask a physician from your church if you can round with him/her one day. Remember, private physicians were trained at some time by academicians and so, most of the time, they will consider it a privilege to teach students. You might consider challenging a Christian physician whom you respect to disciple you while you are in college.

> Discipling is the process by which we enable another person to grow as a disciple of Jesus Christ. . . . Discipling is never a one-way channel by which we impart Christian knowledge or experience "down" to a somewhat less endowed person. Rather, discipleship is a deeply mutual experience in which two people build each other in Christ.[1]

You might think that no physician alive would bother with your request. But beware—the one you ask just might accept!

4. Work with a service organization.

Organizations such as Multiple Sclerosis Society, Diabetes Foundation, and Cerebral Palsy Society can inform you about a number of health-related issues. Working with other organizations such as crisis pregnancy centers and Alcoholics Anonymous can expose you to experiences where physical and spiritual health intersect. Set up an appointment to introduce yourself. See if there is room for a volunteer.

Research

Being involved in laboratory research is a definite advantage in qualifying for medical school. It is not absolutely necessary for admission; it is an opportunity, however, for you to really stand out from other applicants. Remember, the members of the admissions committee are all academic physicians, which means in today's world they are probably involved with research. If they are interested in research, how much more favorable are you as an applicant if you too are interested in research? Some really impressive interviews may revolve around your undergraduate research work.

Another, perhaps more meaningful benefit of conducting research is that one learns the scientific method. There is a distinct discipline involved in understanding and asking the right questions, designing and organizing methods to answer those questions, and observing, analyzing, and interpreting the data accurately. As a physician, you will need to learn how to read scientific literature critically, for in truth, not all science is good science. Many published claims are in fact false and the more of a critical thinker you are, the more apt you will be to see flaws in scientific and medical literature. Research will assist you in honing these very important critical thinking skills.

The final reason I recommend participating in research is the opportunity to appreciate the wonder and glory of the handiwork of God. Some may see the mighty hand of God across the face of the grandest mountain; I see it in the complexity of DNA. One often wonders why such a mighty God is so concerned about man, who is here today and gone tomorrow. David said it in this manner:

Highlight #2

Get experience by volunteering or rounding with a physician from your church.

When I consider your heavens, the work of your fingers, the moon and the stars, which you have set in place, what is man that you are mindful of him, the son of man that you care for him? . . . O LORD, our Lord, how majestic is your name in all the earth! (Ps. 8:3-4, 9)

Highlight #3

Consider investing some time in research.

It is a humbling yet tremendous feeling to know that the God of such might is a God who loves us enough to die for us! To ponder and query the complexity of life in a scientific fashion only deepens this awesome awareness of God's love.

If you have decided to involve yourself in research, the first question that naturally pops up is, How will I find the time to do it? Admittedly, time is already hard to come by in college, but here are some suggestions that I found helpful.

Ways to Get Research Experience

1. Schedule it as a course.

Some departments will allow you to schedule a research project with them and receive credit hours. This accomplishes two purposes: you receive an opportunity to do research, and you're free to take fewer courses for that semester—thus you gain more time. Talk to your premedical counselor, undergraduate advisor, or specific faculty members who design and teach core premedical curricula regarding opportunities for research.

2. Apply for student work scholarships.

If you receive a student work scholarship and request a laboratory assistant position, you will both get paid (nice!) and get experience. The best part of it, however, is that since the professor you will be working for is not directly paying you, you have more flexibility. This means he/she will let you study before tests, go home if there is nothing to do, and so on. This way you can be as involved as you want in research—doing high-powered work or observation and questioning (and washing dishes, of course!).

3. Use your summer for research.

Spending your summers doing research is a great way to

take the pressure off during your peak study seasons, assuming you do not go to summer school. You may even want to do a project at another university just to get a vacation of sorts.

Remember, admissions committees are not expecting Nobel-quality work. You may not get a paper or abstract out of your research, and that is all right. The purpose is simply to show the committee that you are interested in and capable of performing and understanding basic science and/or clinical research.

Honor Societies

There are more honor societies than one would care to count. They typically are organizations that recognize superior students and provide them a vehicle through which to serve. Honor societies such as Phi Beta Kappa and Phi Kappa Phi are perhaps the most prestigious, but that varies from college to college.

Most schools have a premedical honor society that provides premedical students information regarding medicine as a profession, the medical school application process, scholarships, and so on. It is not necessary that one becomes an officer of this society, but most medical school applicants will at least have some cursory affiliation with the premedical honor society.

The question of whether to load one's résumé with honor society after honor society comes up. I once spoke with my dean of students regarding this issue and her advice was this: Admission committee members will see a list of eight honor societies and know that you could not have been active in all eight. You may have been active in one or two, but it is simply impossible to be involved with six to eight organizations. They will know, therefore, that you are résumé "padding." On the other hand, generally speaking, most committee members look favorably on a list of honor societies, so it is better than no societies at all. Ultimately, whether to "pad" or not is up to the individual and how comfortable he or she is with it. As for me, I confess that I had compiled a list of honor societies I had joined, half of which I was not at all involved in. My opinion was that it was an accomplishment just to be invited and that the only way to record this accomplishment was to join—active involvement was and is only an option.

Highlight #4
Get involved with the premedical honor society.

Christian Medical and Dental Society-Premed

There exists a valuable and creative opportunity to gain valuable health-care experience, develop leadership qualities, and enjoy Christian fellowship all at the same time. CMDS-Premed is committed to preparing the Christian premed student—intellectually, spiritually, and ethically—to become a physician. They are also committed to creating an atmosphere for fellowship and Christian service for students.

CMDS-Premed is a efficient resource in that it meets multiple needs of Christian premed students all at the same time. It provides the contacts and experiences with physicians and health care much sought after by premed students. And it creates an atmosphere to enjoy fellowship and an outlet of service. If you want to know more about founding a chapter of this organization (thereby developing leadership skills while serving the Lord), please refer to the Appendix in this book.

Medical School Essay

Your medical school essay(s) will be the summation of your involvement in all of these previous activities, the written synthesis of your experience and personal qualities. You will be presenting your life lessons, your dreams, your hopes, and your accomplishments. In short, you will be presenting yourself, your heart, to the admissions committee on a sheet of paper.

Don't underestimate the importance of the essay—it may be the only component of your application where in one fell swoop you convince a particular member of the admissions committee to champion your cause.

Most essay questions are fairly open-ended and therefore allow you freedom to say what you want. Use the essay to explain why you chose medicine, discuss your particular strengths and weaknesses, and affirm that you will be a compassionate and dedicated physician. The essay does not have to be long; in fact, some of the strongest ones are rather short and to the point. People appreciate economy of words.

Ways to Write a Better Essay

1. Present your strengths.
This seems obvious. Do not be bashful; let the committee know where you are strong. It is not necessary or helpful to be egotistical, but remember that you have God-given qualities. Be proud of them and let the committee know it.

2. Avoid "Christianese."
You are not compromising your faith by doing this. In fact, it shows a certain level of spiritual and emotional maturity to find creative ways to share truth without using religious jargon.

3. Avoid "red flags."
An easy way to receive a negative review from a committee member is to appear caustic, bombastic, or arrogant through your essay. This is especially true regarding such controversial topics as abortion and end-of-life issues. In fact, if at all possible, avoid these topics in your essays so that committee members will not be able to categorize you even before they meet you. A five-hundred-word medical school essay is not the appropriate forum for a soapbox speech.

4. Be creative.
Committee members will read hundreds, possibly thousands, of essays during the year. At some point, they all sound alike. Do not write an essay just outlining all of your accomplishments (a résumé will serve the same purpose); write one that will capture their imaginations. But be careful not to appear eccentric. Since it is often difficult to distinguish between bizarre and creative—creativity is so subjective—ask many people to read your essay and give their honest opinions. Does your creative "gimmick" simply go too far or is it appropriate?

4. Be neat.
Let your family or friends proofread your essay. If you have a word processor, use your spell checker. To submit obvious mistakes will convey to the admissions committee that you did not spend much time on your application and therefore did not regard it as very important.

Highlight #5

In your medical-school essay:

• *Present your strengths.*

• *Avoid "Christianese."*

• *Avoid "red flags."*

• *Be creative.*

• *Be neat.*

Expect these questions:

- Who or what influenced you to pursue medicine as a career?
- Describe medical- and research-related experiences and awards.
- Indicate unusual factors or circumstances in your education.
- Write a two-page autobiography about yourself, your family, and your development.
- What led you to apply to _____?

Following are a couple of essays from very successful friends of mine who are now reputable physicians. These creative efforts present the applicants' strengths while avoiding religious jargon and controversial issues. It is important to develop and stay true to your own style; these are simply examples of two essays that were well received.

Essay One

In the few precious moments allotted to us in life, we must strive for excellence. We must dare to dream. We must play to win. But ironically it is not the attainment of the ultimate goal that makes every struggle worth its toil; it is the pursuit itself. For in such a venture lies the beauty of life—the joy of kin, the growth of awareness and every little daisy-lined milepost along the way.

But however precious life is, it is twice as transient. Like a patch of withering grass, our inherent frailty soon gives way to a stronger and bolder overture—death. It is because of this reality that I will dedicate myself to preserving the most precious and the most fragile commodity ever created—life.

The reasons for my choice of professions are twofold. The first is pragmatic; the second is personal. I shall begin with the latter. Most recently, I have suffered through the loss of my best friend. His death, serving as a primary impetus, compels me to cherish and to esteem that which I have always taken for granted. Coupled with that event is the slow and emotionally painful deterioration of another close friend who has multiple sclerosis. It is the helplessly inept feeling that I possess in regards to those I love that motivates me to pursue medicine. I realize that I will never be able to annihilate death, nor will I always be able to preserve life. But again, it is not the attainment of the ultimate goal that makes every struggle worth its toil; it is the pursuit itself. It is not my purpose upon entering medicine to heal all of those I encounter; it is in the attempt to do so with all patience and understanding where the nobility lies.

My second reason for choosing medicine lies in the fact that my fascinations in academia have almost exclusively been in the areas of the life sciences. Growing up, I knew no other life as my father is a professor of biochemistry and my mother is a professor of microbiology. Peculiarly, I did not want to know any other life. I love science.

But it is not for pure science that I enter medical school. It is for people. People, people, people. It is because of people and the lives lost that I will pursue medicine, and it is because of people and the lives saved that I will practice medicine.

And perhaps, I will gather a few daisies on the way.

Essay Two

During the past three years, I underwent nine laser treatments to eradicate pigmentation in my facial port wine birthmark. Through the course of these treatments I comprehended the temporary pain a patient must endure to achieve physical well-being. I also perceived that the physician provides a valuable humanitarian service not only in the physical sense but in an emotional one as well. As a beneficiary of my family physician's compassion, I have incorporated sympathetic ideals of my own and have been inspired to pursue family medicine. This decision was not made hastily as its development has been taking place for the past decade.

At twelve years of age I was taken to a clinic with a sore arm and my family doctor sympathetically and succinctly diagnosed my fractured arm as if he wielded "x-ray vision." On numerous occasions I have admired the bedside manner of family physicians as a practitioner's "shadow," giving me further exposure to this profession. In 1990, while I was recuperating from a laser treatment, both my sister and father underwent emergency surgery. This stressful period of my life reaffirmed my desire to assist families in need of physical and emotional healing while confirming my abilities to compassionately deal with multiple problematic situations regardless of my physical disposition.

In my role as church youth group leader, I also learned how to administer compassion to troubled teens. This position required a superior level of responsibility with regard to the needs and desires of others.

Most recently, I was honored with the position of a Farrington Scholar. I gained a firsthand appreciation of the rigors of independent scientific research through an investigation of epidermal growth factor. However, the experience only served to confirm my decision to pursue an education in medicine rather than in postgraduate academia because research lacks the humanitarian aspect of compassion and personal communication that I find so imperative to my future as a family practitioner.

An analysis of my background has given me the direction and an impetus to be of service to families who need a caring, attentive and competent physician. I will exemplify these attributes because these qualities have motivated me and will perpetuate my future professional development.

Medical School Interview

This is your last hurdle! The interview serves two purposes: it lets the medical school see you and lets you see the medical school. Most students forget the latter and simply see the interview as a contest of sorts between them and the other applicants. Don't make this mistake.

First and foremost, medical schools want to see individuals that they can work with. They will have to teach you and trust you to take care of patients for the next four years. They will look for mature, dependable, and humane individuals. I have heard of interviews where the interview was just casual discussion about athletics and music because what the interviewer was looking for was someone who was "normal."

Some schools, however, look for individuals who will perform with grace under pressure. They will press you in your interview and ask you very difficult questions—often questions that they do not expect a college student to know how to answer. The object of their query is not so much the quality of the answer but the manner and poise with which it is returned. Smile, be confident, think quickly on your feet . . . and don't forget to relax—God is there with you. He commands His people:

> Be strong and courageous. Do not be terrified; do not be discouraged, for the LORD your God will be with you wherever you go. (Josh. 1:9)

Tips for a Better Interview

1. Rehearse the interview.
Ask a friend to role-play with you. Take this seriously; I assure you the real interview will be a solemn event. Give your friend a random list of questions as well as a copy of your application so he/she may ask you questions from it as well. You will be surprised at how much more poised you are when fielding questions if you have already done it at least once.

2. Review your application.
Reread your AMCAS and secondary application, because most interviewers simply read straight from your application and ask about a certain honor you received or point of interest in your essay. They may ask for clarification or elaboration. Be prepared to comment briefly (a sentence or two) on each item on your application, drawing out a particular God-given strength of yours.

3. Articulate for yourself why you should attend that school.
If you cannot explain clearly why you should attend that school, you certainly will not convince the interviewer. If Billy Boudreaux from Houma, Louisiana, does not know why he should attend Yale Medical School instead of Louisiana State, neither will the interviewer.

Highlight #6
For your medical-school interview:

• Perform a practice interview.

• Review your application.

• Articulate for yourself why you should attend that school.

• Say what you are good at saying.

• Talk with a private physician.

• Ask relevant questions.

• Send thank-you notes.

4. Say what you are good at saying.

I have a friend who is a state-level politician who seems able or willing to talk about only seven or eight different things. He uses the same phrases, the same jokes, and even the same inflections in his voice each time. Every question or conversation is somehow cleverly rerouted back to these seven or eight main points about which he is so apt in communicating both substantively and stylistically. So it should be in your interview. Talk about what you know; just reroute the conversation to one of the topics you are familiar with. You will sound absolutely brilliant! This means, of course, that you know something about seven or eight different and relevant topics like healthcare reform, what a good doctor is, and what your experience in the hospital has been like on a personal and professional level. This knowledge is acquired slowly; begin now by talking to people, thinking about it, and reciting to yourself a knowledgeable answer.

5. Talk with a private physician beforehand.

This is related to the last suggestion, of course. Pick the brain of a physician about current issues regarding healthcare delivery, ethics, insurance, and so on. These are not topics that premedical students are usually informed about but physicians often are. Understanding the healthcare problems of today will help you in your interview.

6. Ask relevant questions.

The interviewer will typically end the conversation with, "Do you have any questions for me?" This is an opportunity for you to glean some information for yourself since the interview exists also for your benefit. Interviewers will be impressed with thoughtful questions—you show more interest asking questions than not doing so. (Hint: don't ask, "How did I do in the interview?")

Here are some sample questions:

- What kind of research opportunities (required semesters, elective credits, or funding for summer research) do medical students have?
- What is (the city) like?
- How would you characterize the student body makeup?

- What sort of financial aid is available? Scholarships?

7. Expect these questions:

- Why do you want to go into medicine?
- What is wrong with medicine today? How would you fix it?
- What are your strengths and weaknesses?
- How do you handle stress?
- Who are three people in history you would like to meet?
- What do you do for fun?
- Are you interested in primary care? Surgery? Specialties?
- Tell me about (anything you've written in your application).
- What has been your biggest regret to date?
- Where do you see yourself in ten years?

8. Send thank-you notes.

Remember to send a thank-you note to whoever interviewed you. Be cordial, but don't overdo it. Let the interviewer know you appreciated the opportunity to see the school and to meet with him/her personally. Notes are a nice added touch.

The Christian Connection

There exists a genuine and valid concern over how to present ourselves as Christians during the application and interview process. Will we be discriminated against if we are vocal about our beliefs? Dare we stand up for what we believe lest we "compromise our faith"? How do we answer the hard questions that deal with abortion, contraception, end-of-life issues, honesty/integrity, and so on?

A recent study suggested that there appears to be an overall apprehension in interviewers and admission committee members about admitting any candidate with strong religious beliefs.[2] Gunn *et al,* reviewed written comments by admissions committee members from an unnamed medical school who had interviewed a number of Christians. Here are some telling comments from that investigation:

Highlight #7

Christian medical students must present themselves as mature academically, emotionally, and spiritually.

Case 1

In discussing various issues related to medicine—especially ethical and moral issues—I felt that her viewpoint was rather narrow or rigid and that she has not thought through the issues very well. She is strongly religious and called herself a "Christian." When I asked her about National Health Insurance, she simply stated that socialized medicine would be a hindrance to the American people—and did not really elaborate on this. When I asked her about her stand on abortion, she simply said that she would never perform one, and would try very hard to talk a prospective patient out of having an abortion, even if this was a rape victim. Although these are sensitive issues and people's opinions vary a lot, I felt that Ms. 1's answers were preformed rather than logically sound.

Case 2

For someone who has had so much experience of a medical person's life-style, I found Mr. 2 to be immature, and quite rigid in his thinking. He presents as a smiling, clean-cut, well-dressed young man, but he was somewhat at a loss for words, and I could not meaningfully discuss many issues with him. His interests seemed to be exclusively in outdoor sports and in church activities. Although he had taken a good deal of history, government, English and French in school, I found it hard to discuss current events or controversial topics with him. . . . I was somewhat concerned by Mr. 2's attitude toward religion and medicine. . . . Mr. 2 insisted upon taking a highly moralistic stance. For example, he said that when advising a twenty-five-year-old woman about contraception, he would first want her to convince him that her activities were "moral." I found this attitude very disturbing. . . .

Are admissions committee members really prejudiced against Christians as a whole or do these represent isolated comments that do not reflect a general trend? My experience, although limited, is the latter.

There are two reasons why. First, admissions committees are looking for mature men and women—academically, emotionally, and spiritually. Being a Christian in and of itself does not make one instantly mature in any way. In fact, it appears to me that the individuals in these cases were quite the opposite in their thought lives. They perhaps knew the truth of Scripture but only on a level of canned answers and religious jargon. The truth is defensible and reasonable! We simply need to take the time to look at all sides of issues and present our stances only after deep thought—and with savvy intelligence and compassion. It is my hunch that at the core of the inability to present ourselves as mature, thoughtful Christians is often spiritual pride. The college years, meaningful and precious as they are, are often earmarked by a youthful exuberance and zeal which lends itself to arrogance and carelessness. We think we have all of the answers and so we take great pride in espousing the truth—even in a haughty and sometimes bombastic manner. We take for granted the fact that though we speak the truth that there exist issues of relevance at depths that we have never comprehended. And so our loose, almost flippant dealing with these sensitive issues is not respected by nonbelievers.

This is not discrimination! This is simply the result of a believer's inability to present himself or herself as a wise, thoughtful, and mature individual. This should not happen. Jesus said to His disciples,

> I am sending you out like sheep among wolves. Therefore be as shrewd as snakes and as innocent as doves. (Matt. 10:16)

Solomon taught:

> A gentle answer turns away wrath, but a harsh word stirs up anger. The tongue of the wise commends knowledge, but the mouth of the fool gushes folly. (Prov. 15:1-2)

A second reason why I believe that Christians are not discriminated against by and large is the reality that many Christians are entering the field of medicine. If prejudice really existed, great organizations such as Christian Medical and Dental Society and many, many healthcare missions organizations wouldn't thrive. There is an undercurrent of spirituality in the healing arts that even a nonbe-

Highlight #8

There is an understanding of spirituality in the healing arts that even a nonbeliever recognizes to some degree.

liever recognizes to some degree. One cannot go a day without seeing pastors, priests, or hospital chaplains visiting and praying with their patients.

This is still a country of great freedom. We are free to worship our God and express this worship openly. Medicine, perhaps even more than other professions, is tolerant of spirituality as even the casual observer would readily admit to the spiritual component in suffering, disease, health, and healing. Rather than being victims of discrimination, we are recipients of a tremendous amount of freedom. It's not always perfect or absolute, but it is a privilege nonetheless.

Sometimes, though, despite a mature, thoughtful, and reasonable presentation of our beliefs, we will be misunderstood or judged harshly by nonbelievers—that is okay. We are promised in Scripture that the world will judge us fools and that God allows these difficult times for our own good (James 1:2-4). But whatever suffering or difficulties we may encounter as ambassadors for Christ, we are also promised grace that will suffice (2 Cor. 12:9). May we all be shrewd as serpents and innocent as doves; let us present ourselves as thoughtful, mature, and humble people. And let us trust in God to overcome the potential prejudices of the world and grant us the wisdom and truth to represent Him.

Difficult Questions

There are a handful of trip-wire questions that prospective medical students should be prepared for. Because they are often political or religious in nature, they can be intimidating to answer. Do not fear these questions—they will come. It is just a matter of when and how often. Be prepared so you are not startled. Do your best and leave the rest to God.

Here are a few of the most oft-asked questions and some potential answers to them. These are but a few thoughts that you may work on and modify as you deem appropriate. Let these be a starting point for you.

Question: What would you do if a fourteen-year old girl came to you for an abortion?
Answer: As a Christian I believe that God gives life and that it is precious. And I believe that as a physician it is my role to help and extend love toward my

patients. Therefore, I would not try to enforce my beliefs on a young girl, but instead encourage her and help her in any way I could to make a wise decision about her baby, her body, and her future. This might mean helping her contact local organizations that support women through pregnancies physically, emotionally, financially, and spiritually. It might mean putting her in touch with other women who have been in her situation who can counsel her through this very tough time in her life. I would do everything in my power to help her during her pregnancy.

Question: What if she still wants the abortion?
Answer: I might inform her, with understanding and gentleness, of the dangers emotionally and physically of abortions.

Question: And what if she still wants an abortion after all of this?
Answer: The reality is, I cannot force her to carry out the pregnancy; but neither can I perform a procedure that goes against my beliefs. I would not perform the procedure, even if I knew the girl would simply have it done elsewhere.

I must add, however, that even if she were to go ahead with the decision that in no way would this affect how I viewed or treated her. I would still want to be her physician and would treat her with respect and dignity. What she does or does not do should not and does not affect how I see her. If she needs me down the road, I will be there. I will not abandon her because she does something against my beliefs.

Question: What would you do if you caught your best friend cheating on an exam?
Answer: This is a very difficult question because it pits honesty/integrity as a student against trustworthiness as a friend. I cannot tell you that my answer is definitive since perhaps the situation itself may present the obvious answer. Generally speaking, though, I believe I would confront my friend with every intention of helping him. I would act from love and concern, not a sense of "justice" or self-righteousness.

I would suspect that his choice to cheat is a sign of deeper problems. I would want to know if my friend was motivated by academic struggles or personal problems, and how those might be resolved constructively. I would want to know how I could help. I think that is my responsibility as his friend.

Your responses to these and other tough questions, as well as the experience you obtain and the eagerness you exhibit, will convince a medical school of your heartfelt intention to become an outstanding doctor.

Points to Ponder

1. Have you had any experience with the healthcare profession or research? What impressions do you have?

2. Have you ever been discriminated against as a Christian? To what extent?

3. What do you think is the wisest way to present yourself in your medical school application and interview?

4. How will you answer the tough questions regarding abortion and end-of-life issues?

Notes

1. E. Stanley Ott, *The Joy of Discipling* (Grand Rapids, MI: Zondervan Publishing, 1989), 38.

2. A. E. Gunn, G. O. Zenner Jr., "Religious discrimination in the selection of medical students: a case study," *Issues in Law and Medicine* 11:4 (1989), 353-78.

Part III
The Future

Chapter 6
Myths and Pitfalls of
Medical School

*It is a good thing to learn caution from the misfortunes
of others.*
—**Publilius Syrus**

*Experience is a hard teacher because she gives the test first,
the lesson afterwards.*
—**Vernon Saunders Law**

Myths of Medical School

1. I'll fail medical school.

2. I can expect a nasty competitive spirit in medical school.

3. It's impossible to have an outside life while in medical school.

4. I won't have time for personal devotions while in medical school.

I t is common to see a movie, popular television show, book, or interview that casts some kind of stereotype on medical education in the nineties. Consequently everybody has some idea, usually inaccurate, of what it is like to be a medical student or resident. The result of the entertainment industry's capitalizing on society's interest in the lives and times of budding physicians is that some myths have been created while real pitfalls are ignored. Here are a few of the significant misunderstandings propagated today.

Myths of Medical School

Myth #1
I'll fail medical school.

At exactly 8:00 A.M. on the morning of the first gathering of the very first day of medical school, the dean brought us to attention with a stern voice and said, "Look to your left. Now, look to your right. At graduation, both people will be there—I promise." This was a stark contrast from the more traditional and expected threats that "most of you will flunk." There existed a time when graduate medical education was much more demanding, regimented, and almost militaristic. Medical students and residents were expected to be single, to reside in the hospital day and night, and to live and breathe medicine alone for years—and if they could not cut that they failed the program. Such a time has passed. There is still a lot of hard work, but students, for the most part, simply do not fail medical school. Occasionally there will be a student who needs to repeat a year or who needs to retake national boards, but this is still a very small minority nationally. As a rule, if a student is qualified to get into medical school, he or she is qualified to finish medical school.

Admission committees are very good at selecting applicants who they feel will be capable of the academic load and will excel scholastically. Regardless of how compassionate or altruistic an applicant may be, no admissions committee would ever vote for an applicant they feel is incapable of finishing the work of medical school. Over the past twenty years, attrition due to dismissal has been at or around 1 percent. In fact, two to three times as many students withdraw from medical school themselves than actually fail. Overall attrition rates are between 2 and 3 percent.[1]

Besides a sharp admissions committee that filters out unqualified applicants, there is another reason why medical students generally do not fail medical school. It is because the school itself has a lot invested in its students. Money, time, and the school's reputation are at stake; if the student doesn't graduate and perform well nationally on standardized board exams, this reflects on the school. In fact, it is often thought that medical schools depend on student tuition and fees to survive, but actually the opposite is true. I attended a private medical school; it did not benefit from state funding, so naturally the tuition and fees were much higher. Nevertheless, even with the lofty bill, the total student tuition and fees added up to only 4 percent of the total medical-school operating budget! So it was not our funds that kept the school going, it was the school's funds that kept us going!

Because graduate medical education is expensive and schools have a lot invested in each student, they will go out of their way to assist, encourage, and provide whatever resource is necessary to see that each student meets his or her academic potential. Schools supply plenty of computers, laboratory assistants, quiet study areas, and helpful tutoring sessions just to help students excel.

Highlight #1
Medical students rarely fail medical school.

Myth #2
I can expect a nasty competitive spirit at medical school.

Medical students, again by and large, are simply not competitive in underhanded or unhealthy ways. In fact, I found undergraduate school to be much more competitive than medical school; this is due in part to the fact that most everyone graduates and generally performs well throughout medical school. There is no need to be competitive and no advantage to seeing classmates as enemies. Students are not competing as they were for medical-school admission slots. They are all working for the same goal: to learn the skills of being a good doctor. Many students recognize

Highlight #2

Brutal competition is usually not a factor at medical school.

the advantage of working together and helping each other get through the work. It is this camaraderie and teamwork that made medical school so special for me. Lifelong friendships were knit during late nights when each person in a study group was assigned a topic to teach the rest of the group to save time. Students worked together in a spirit of teamwork to accomplish the goal—of finishing, not failing. Although I cannot substantiate this claim by way of some large, multicenter randomized study, I did perform a small informal study of my own to see if my hunch was right. I asked ten friends who all went to different under-graduate and medical school programs this question: Which was more competitive—undergraduate or medical school? Nine out of ten said that undergraduate school was more competitive in the sense that students were more keenly aware of and cared more about how others did in comparison to themselves. However, most qualified that with a caveat that although the competition in medical school was less, the work itself was harder. Less competi-tion does not mean less work.

Myth #3

It is impossible to have an outside life while in medical school.

I recently watched a popular television show about resi-dents and medical students where at the end of a terribly hectic day (as if they are all like that), the medical student and the resident prepare to go home. Each has the day off. They look at one another and ask, "What are you going to do today?" Confused by the apparent surprise of having time to spare, each answers, "I don't know." The inference and stereotype is, of course, that residents and medical students have no life outside the hospital and that given a free day all of them would have absolutely no idea what to do with it. They're dedicated to the profession to the extent that they cultivate no outside interests.

I would like to add that this stereotype is not just the fault of the entertainment industry. Physicians and students alike enjoy propagating this myth simply because they are proud of their dedication and commitment to a rigorous profession. Most who exhibit such pride would have you believe that they are victims of the medical education system, that they have no control over medicine becoming such a dominant force in their lives. After all, it is not their fault that they are so single-minded. Medicine demands and exacts such dedication.

In this same television show, medicine and the pursuit of it destroys marriages and relationships. The writing portrays the characters and their motives as noble and altruistic, whereas spouses and family members seem ignorant of and unsympathetic to the demands of medicine. They simply do not understand what the profession *requires* of their loved ones, so they become impatient and cold. And so the stereotype continues: the necessary and endless dedication to medicine victimizes the true heroes— the physicians and students—by destroying their personal lives.

It is true, however, that graduate medical education can inculcate, very subtly, an unhealthy commitment to the profession—but only if one lets it. Over the course of years it can reinforce the idea that the only treasure in life is medicine. This is true, however, of any profession. If we are not on guard, medicine will present itself first as an acquaintance, then a friend, then a lover, and finally a master. If we allow ourselves onto this slippery slope, we will find that we do not have time for a "life" because medicine will be consuming all of our energies: our minds, wills, and emotions. Jesus said:

Highlight #3
Medical students can and must set aside time for "a life."

> Every kingdom divided against itself will be ruined, and every city or household divided against itself will not stand. (Matt. 12:25)

> No one can serve two masters. Either he will hate the one and love the other, or he will be devoted to the one and despise the other. (Matt. 6:24)

If we don't actively make other choices, medicine will entrench itself as our one master in life.

The truth remains, however, that medicine does not have to become our master. Everyone is busy, but busyness does not justify mixed priorities. One does not *have* time for a "life"; one simply has to *make* time. It is important to purposefully set aside time for your family, your friends, and for yourself—which may be in the form of exercise, recreation, and rest. These are "margins" that we must

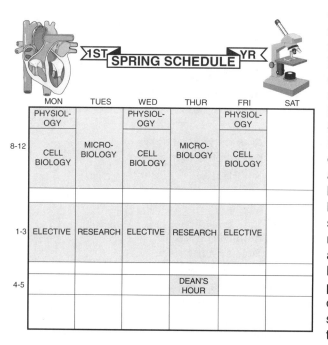

	MON	TUES	WED	THUR	FRI	SAT
8-12	BIOCHEM	GROSS ANATOMY	BIOCHEM	GROSS ANATOMY	BIOCHEM	GROSS ANATOMY
	PSYCH		PSYCH		PSYCH	
1-3	ELECTIVE	GROSS ANATOMY	ELECTIVE	GROSS ANATOMY	ELECTIVE	
4-5				DEAN'S HOUR		

	MON	TUES	WED	THUR	FRI	SAT
8-12	PHYSIOL-OGY	MICRO-BIOLOGY	PHYSIOL-OGY	MICRO-BIOLOGY	PHYSIOL-OGY	
	CELL BIOLOGY		CELL BIOLOGY		CELL BIOLOGY	
1-3	ELECTIVE	RESEARCH	ELECTIVE	RESEARCH	ELECTIVE	
4-5				DEAN'S HOUR		

build into our lives if we are to succeed. If we do not actively seek time to spend on these important things, the complex demands of medicine will be too difficult to overcome. Therefore, we must choose to make other things important by granting them time. Jesus says that "where your treasure is, there your heart will be also" (Luke 12:34). We choose where we will invest our hearts.

I must put in a disclaimer: as I mentioned earlier, one may occasion-ally need to work eighty- to one-hundred- hour work-weeks. There are seasons in medical school in which one may find it very difficult, even impossible, to build margins into his/her life for family, friends, exercise, recreation, and rest. This does not estab-lish forever medicine's dominance in the student's life. It is an occasional demand you must expect and plan for, by making the best of the times you don't have to work such a heavy schedule. Medicine does not become overpowering at a certain hour-per-week limit, but when it takes the place of God in the heart of man. Medical students should work hard during these seasons of medical school, working "as if unto the Lord," trusting that this, as all seasons do, will pass and once again that they will be able to build margins in their lives. It is trouble only if you realize that you are volunteering for these seasons at the expense of your family, friends, and health.

Let me repeat: that sort of schedule is *not* normal for a medical student. Most medical schools are four-year programs; you spend the first two years in the classroom for basic science instruction and the last two years in the hospital for clinical instruction. During your first two years, classes usually start 8:00 A.M. and last until noon. Other days, where there is a lab or small group, classes might extend until 3:00 or 4:00 P.M. Pictured are sample schedules from a local medical school broken up into different semesters for the first and second years of medical school.

Typically, students study most nights, but most of the students I knew (myself included) rarely studied after 11:00 or midnight. There are usually no classes on the weekends and time exists for medical-school mixers,

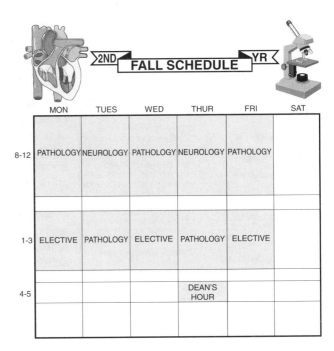

2ND FALL SCHEDULE YR

	MON	TUES	WED	THUR	FRI	SAT
8-12	PATHOLOGY	NEUROLOGY	PATHOLOGY	NEUROLOGY	PATHOLOGY	
1-3	ELECTIVE	PATHOLOGY	ELECTIVE	PATHOLOGY	ELECTIVE	
4-5				DEAN'S HOUR		

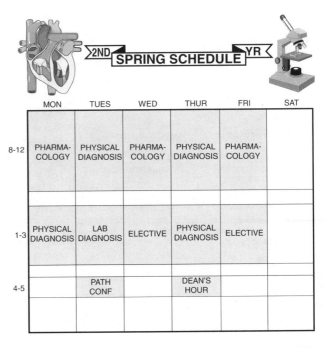

2ND SPRING SCHEDULE YR

	MON	TUES	WED	THUR	FRI	SAT
8-12	PHARMA-COLOGY	PHYSICAL DIAGNOSIS	PHARMA-COLOGY	PHYSICAL DIAGNOSIS	PHARMA-COLOGY	
1-3	PHYSICAL DIAGNOSIS	LAB DIAGNOSIS	ELECTIVE	PHYSICAL DIAGNOSIS	ELECTIVE	
4-5		PATH CONF		DEAN'S HOUR		

THIRD YEAR

JUNE-AUGUST **PEDIATRICS**	PEDIATRIC WARDS -6 WKS PEDIATRIC CLINIC - 2 WKS
AUGUST-OCTOBER **PSYCHIATRY**	PSYCH WARDS - 4 WKS PSYCH CLINIC - 2 WKS NEUROLOGY CONSULT - 2 WKS
OCTOBER-DECEMBER **OBSTETRICS GYNECOLOGY**	OB CLINIC - 2 WKS OB DELIVERY - 2 WKS GYN CLINIC - 2 WKS GYN WARDS - 2 WKS
JANUARY-MARCH **INTERNAL MEDICINE**	MEDICINE WARDS - 6 WKS MEDICINE CLINIC - 6 WKS
MARCH-MAY **SURGERY**	GENERAL SURGERY - 4 WKS SURGERY ELECTIVE - 2 WKS SURGERY ELECTIVE - 2 WKS

FOURTH YEAR

JUNE **PEDIATRICS**	DECEMBER **OFF MONTH/INTERVIEWS**
JULY **TRAUMA SURGERY**	JANUARY **MEDICAL INTENSIVE CARE**
AUGUST **EMERGENCY MEDICINE**	FEBRUARY **OUTPATIENT MEDICINE**
SEPTEMBER **CARDIOLOGY**	MARCH **INFECTIOUS DISEASE**
OCTOBER **DERMATOLOGY**	APRIL **OFF MONTH**
NOVEMBER **RADIOLOGY**	MAY **GRADUATION!**

athletic events, or time alone to do chores or rest. However, around midterms or final exams, both weekends and nights became intense periods of fairly constant study.

The third year of medical school is perhaps busier than the other three because students spend a great deal of time in the hospital with patients, but it is still not unmanageable. There are five or six primary clerkships that students rotate through, usually in two- to three-month blocks. They include internal medicine, obstetrics and gynecology, pediatrics, psychiatry, and surgery. Pictured are sample schedule of third- and fourth-year clerkships.

Certain rotations will require you to be in from only 8:00 A.M. to 5:00 P.M., after which you may do anything you want: read, go out, or sleep. Other more difficult rotations (which vary from school to school) probably have you in the hospital anywhere from 5:00 A.M. to 6:00 A.M. to pre-round on your patients (see them, examine them, and write notes on them). You may leave the hospital anywhere from 4:00 P.M. to 8:00 P.M. most days. You will also be on call periodically (usually every fourth night), which means that you stay in the hospital overnight and take care of patients. Call nights can be difficult as you may not sleep more than a few hours.

Your fourth year of medical school has a lot of flexibility built in so that you can fill out residency applications and interview and do clerkships at other schools. Most fourth-year blocks are broken up into one-month rotations and most schools require from eight to ten blocks to fulfill fourth-year requirements. Many fourth-year rotations last just 8:00 A.M. to 5:00 P.M., but others are more difficult with call nights.

> ## Highlight #4
> *The spiritual life must be grace- and not performance-based.*

Put another way, there are plenty of gaps in your schedule in which to exercise, eat with friends, go out on dates, and even get married (which I did). In fact, I found the first semester of medical school, where I concentrated on only anatomy and biochemistry, to be the least stressful semester of my life! One's relationships with God and with people should not and will not be affected by medical school itself unless you allow them to be. There is room for "a life" in medical school; you have the power and freedom to create it—in the heart *and* in the Day-timer.

Myth #4
I won't have time for personal devotions in medical school.

At first, this seems related to the previous myth and therefore repetitious. Actually this myth is more complex than it appears. First of all, there will be time for personal devotions or quiet times in medical school as long as you make it; it is one of those essentials worthy of our continued attention.

The issue isn't really whether or not we have time; the issue is why we have quiet times at all. There is a tendency in the compulsive community of the premedical and medical student to see the Christian life as just another performance-based area in life where he is both judged and rewarded by his accomplishments. There lurks the belief that we have a "good" spiritual day if we have shared the gospel, had a productive quiet time, and prayed, and a "bad" spiritual day if we have not. On a "good" day, the thinking goes, God will "bless" my efforts to be like Him and be a good witness for Him and He is generally pleased with me as a son or daughter; but on a "bad" day, things may go awry, relationships may become strained, stress levels will increase, and God is generally frowning on me. We desire to walk through life compiling a string of "good" days so that we can reach that vague and arbitrary number of "good" days when God deems us "faithful." We know that when we go to heaven that should we present a sufficient number of "good" days, God will say to us, "Well done, good and faithful servant."

The tendency to live and believe in such a way is especially prevalent for those of us who are so used to working for everything we get. Against the backdrop of such a performance-based world as medicine, it is difficult to accept that God loves us freely and that He died for sinners. It is hard to imagine the vast chasm between His holiness and our sinfulness because we are too used to getting what we deserve. This mindset does not reflect a biblical understanding of the Christian life. This is not freedom; this is slavery. What, then, is the Christian life?

The answer, of course, goes back to the gospel of grace. St. Augustine defined grace as God's generous and unmerited attention to humanity by which the process of healing the frail, weak, and lost human nature is begun and carried out.[2] The word *gospel* comes from the Greek root *evangelon,* which means "good news." Putting these two words together, then, we see that the gospel of grace is the good news that though we did not merit it, God will see that the real and redeeming Christ transforms us. Put another way, as Dr. Jack Miller, founder of World Harvest Mission, used to say "Cheer up! You are actually worse off than you think! But God's love is greater than you think."

It is easy to nod in agreement to these words, applying them to only nonbelievers who lack conversion. But these words are for Christians too! Believers too often forget that grace is also for them. We think that grace was a factor just for our conversion, but surely now spiritual discipline and moral rigor pave the path to holiness. *This is not so!* Grace began the work of sanctification in you and grace will complete it. Grace is and must be the central force governing our lives as believers. Nobody "outgrows" the gospel; it is for unbelievers and believers alike. In fact, the gospel is of use only once for an unbeliever (conversion) but the gospel is of use time and time again for the believer (transformation). Jerry Bridges, former vice president of The Navigators, put it this way in his book *The Discipline of Grace*:

> The gospel is not only the most important message in all of history; it is the only important message in all of history. Yet we allow thousands of professing Christians to live their entire lives without clearly understanding it and experiencing the joy of living by it.[3]

Paul wrote to the church in Galatia about this very same subject. They heard and eagerly received his message of grace embodied in the gospel. But then Christian Jews came along and tried to pervert the Christian walk into one of grace *and* performance. Paul responded as such:

> I would like to learn just one thing from you: Did you receive the Spirit by observing the law, or by believing what you heard? Are you so foolish? After beginning with the Spirit, are you now trying to attain your goal by human effort? (Gal. 3:2-3)

Paul said that we began (conversion) by the Spirit, by hearing with faith, and that we must be perfected (transformation) in the same manner. We live every day surrounded by grace, which makes God's love absolutely consistent and unchanging whether we feel we have a "good" spiritual day or a "bad" one.

We must learn to preach the gospel to ourselves every day, lest we forget the joy and liberation it brings. The belief in performance-based relationships runs so deep, we need consistent reminding of our position in Christ lest we continue to try to deserve it. It is this need to earn what we already possess in Christ that gets us into trouble. We do this because we forget what we have and who we are—as Martin Luther said, "We leak." We must remember:

> You are a chosen people, a royal priesthood, a holy nation, a people belonging to God, that you may declare the praises of him who called you out of darkness into his wonderful light. Once you were not a people, but now you are the people of God; once you had not received mercy, but now you have received mercy. (1 Peter 2:9-10)

God ordained that we would learn to love Him all the more as we grow in our understanding of what He has done for us. As we see what a tremendous price He paid for us, we see just how much He must love us and thus we love Him all the more.

We as believers need to live each day, few as our days are, with an earnest desire to be filled with and reminded of grace, to understand it more profoundly, and to be empowered by it. May the Spirit of God's grace cover your heart as you live each day purposefully to His glory and honor!

Pitfalls of Medical School

Pitfall #1
Medical students have limited time for relationships.

Pitfalls of Medical School

1. Medical students have limited time for relationships.

2. Medical students feel guilty about having romantic relationships.

3. Marriage is an extra challenge for medical students.

The summer before I started medical school, I participated in a national student conference in Chicago. The organizers of the conference put me in a room with a second-year medical student from the school I was to start in the fall, thinking probably that he would impart many words of wisdom to me. After a brief introduction, he eagerly asked me if I was dating anyone at the time. I told him I was. A smug and knowing look quickly appeared on his face as he raised his right hand, slowly cocked his thumb, and clicked an imaginary stopwatch! This was his way of telling me that it was just a matter of time until the relationship was over. My friend, though not exactly subtle, was correct in his assessment that a romantic relationship is difficult to maintain while in medical school. But it is not, by any stretch of the imagination, impossible.

What is perhaps the most difficult part of relationships in medical school, especially romantic ones, is actually meeting new people. Medical students spend 99 percent of their time with each other, so it is difficult to meet students in other fields by taking part in a church singles group or city-wide coed frisbee football team. In fact, it is not uncommon for medical students to marry each other or marry other hospital staff such as nurses or hospital technicians. This happens because Christian activities involving medical personnel where Christian students can meet other students and the like are well-attended. As proof, six of my classmates recently got married: four of them met their spouses at medical school fellowships, one met his spouse at church, and only one outside those activities!

As I mentioned earlier, there is time for things outside of medicine. It is brief, though. All relationships, including romantic ones, need time and it is important to set it aside for them. This time may be in the form of a phone call, a quick letter/E-mail, a shared meal, or time in the Scriptures and in prayer. Whatever form meetings take, relationships are worth investing in.

I have found that to maximize time in the context of relationships, it is helpful not only to schedule time for people but to take them along in my daily routine. That is, instead of exercising or eating alone, I take a friend. Does a roommate need to do laundry too? Go together. Certainly solitude and reflection are important, but friendships help us keep perspective, among many other benefits, and should be counted as worth the precious commodity of time.

Highlight #5

It is important and necessary to honor relationships with time.

Pitfall #2
Medical students feel guilty about having romantic relationships.

This is extraordinarily common within the Christian community, especially among the more mature Christians, ironically. "Brad" is a friend of mine who became quite fond of another friend of mine, "Ellen." Brad experienced a mixture of both nirvana and guilt about falling in love. He was elated to find a member of the opposite sex to adore and cherish, yet at the same time he felt guilty that he did not possess the same level of emotion for God. "If God is really Lord of my life," he would accuse himself, "why don't I feel this way about Him?" He wondered if Ellen had become more important to him than God. He considered whether he could leave her "if God told me to." As the anxiety grew—the more Brad and Ellen fell in love—the more the questions hounded him. *Am I in idolatry? Is my heart an adulterous one?* Soon, questions led to action and he set imaginary emotional boundaries in his heart.

Brad put himself through unnecessary restrictions. His line of thinking (you may remember this from a previous chapter) was: God must have more of my heart than anything else in this world, and everything else must have less of my heart than God. This is hogwash! God wants all of our hearts, not just 51 percent. Our vision is too limited! Using the list and GIST paradigms again, we remember that God is not at the top of our list of priorities, He *is* the list. He has given us all of the things on the list as gifts to be used to worship Him and change us. They are not enemies of God; they are gifts from God. My spouse does

113

not vie for space in my heart that God alone should have; she is a gift from Him that I love dearly. So it could have been with Brad.

Give yourself the freedom to love your significant other or spouse the best way you know how, in a manner which Christ and the Scriptures teach. There is a common fear that you will love him or her too much. Again, hogwash! You cannot love too much, you can only "love" selfishly *or* in a Christ-like manner. It is not the quantity of emotion or commitment but the quality of each that deems it noble or sinful.

We must realize that emotions are God-given. We are creatures wired by a divine Genius to relate to Him and one another. Trust that emotions are good and proper. Do not feel guilty over them; enjoy them as part of God's providence. Respect, esteem, encourage, and honor your significant other and enjoy the warmth of love as God unfolds His sovereign plan for your life.

Highlight #6

Relationships are a gift from God: don't be afraid to lavish your love in them.

Pitfall #3

Marriage is an extra challenge for medical students.

Understand me here when I say that marriage is a "pitfall" only in the sense that it is more difficult than most would imagine. My comments are not meant as a warning against pursuing a romantic relationship or marriage while in medical school but to encourage you to actively nurture and maintain that relationship. It will take a lot of work while you are dating, and it will take a lot of work after you are married.

For many years now, medical marriages have remained under indictment as physicians are seen as high-risk marriage partners. A number of studies and books were published in the 1970s that suggested a higher rate of divorce and dissatisfaction in medical marriages. Stories floated around of high-powered residencies *bragging* of 100-percent divorce rates. As further evidence of marital dysfunction, it was reported that physicians were also at the highest risk of alcoholism and suicide. What, if it is known at all, is the truth regarding medical marriages?

It appears, in fact, that there is no truth to the notion that physicians divorce at a higher rate. The largest and most accurate study on this subject, published in *The*

Journal of the American Medical Association in 1989, showed that physicians actually have a *lower* divorce rate than the general population.[4] However, the authors of this article clearly delineate the difference between marital stability (proneness to divorce) and marital quality (subjective evaluation of the relationship). In other words, just because a marriage lasts does not mean it's a satisfying relationship.

Other authors, while perhaps admitting statistical significance in a lower divorce rate, believe that physicians have unique problems. Gabbard and Menninger report:

> Many physicians' marriages are characterized by a strategy of postponement. The demands of medical training, the rigors of establishing a practice, and the expectations of colleagues are often used as excuses to avoid emotional intimacy in the marital relationship. Attention to the needs of the marriage is regularly postponed until some indefinite point in the future, resulting in considerable covert marital discord.[5]

Physicians are taught to delay gratification and place work over family. They put off household chores, dates, and even heart-to-heart talks, using the rigors of the profession as an excuse. Eventually a pattern of emotional distance, bitterness, and ultimately despair sets in. It is not uncommon for the spouse of a physician or for the physician him- or herself to feel, twenty years down the line, resentment over this distance and seek someone else who can and will meet their needs.

This issue of "needs" is one that has to be addressed because it so often crops up in marriage. When one talks of needs, one is not referring to shelter, food, and clothing but rather to purpose, love, meaning, wholeness, and intimacy. These are all inner desires that stem from being human. Dr. Larry Crabb says that all inner human desires can be summed up in the words *security* and *significance*. He defines security as "a convinced awareness of being unconditionally and totally loved without needing to change in order to win love, loved by a love that is freely given, that cannot be earned and therefore cannot be lost." Significance is "a realization that I am engaged in a responsibility or job that is truly important, whose results will not evaporate with time but will last through eternity, that fundamen-

Highlight #7

Medical marriages, like all marriages, must be based in grace.

tally involves having a meaningful impact on another person, a job for which I am completely adequate."[6]

God provides His perfect love for our security and adopts us as His children for our significance. God and only God meets our deepest needs. Paul wrote to the church at Ephesus and praised God for giving us all that we need:

> Praise be to the God and Father of our Lord Jesus Christ, who has blessed us in the heavenly realms with every spiritual blessing in Christ. For he chose us in him before the creation of the world to be holy and blameless in his sight. In love he predestined us to be adopted as his sons through Jesus Christ, in accordance with his pleasure and will—to the praise of his glorious grace, which he has freely given us in the One he loves. (Eph. 1:3-6)

God has blessed us *with every spiritual blessing*. We are complete in Him. All of our deepest longings for unconditional love and existential meaning are met in who we are in Christ. Only God can fill our inner needs for security and significance, and any attempt to look to a human being for these will always end in frustration and disappointment. No spouse can be what God alone can be. Therefore, it is inappropriate of one spouse to expect it of the other. Nor is it appropriate for one spouse to think that he or she can and should meet those needs, for again, only God can. The first step in preventing marital discord is to recognize this.

Physicians and their spouses will not find true satisfaction in each other, in their work, in their children, or anything other than Jesus Christ Himself. Admittedly, there is true pain in bad marriages, even in Christian marriages. But one's security and significance do not depend on and are not related to one's happiness. It is entirely possible to find true satisfaction in a relationship with Christ and yet experience every bit of pain and suffering that comes with living in a fallen and sinful world.

In fact, it is only when spouses allow God to meet their deepest needs that they themselves can become the spouses that God wants them to be. It is the deep knowledge that they are loved perfectly by God that allows spouses to forgive each other when hurt or rejection enters the relationship. There is a certain desire in all physicians to have the "perfect" doctor's wife or husband. This spouse is one who will entertain, be witty, sharp, and attractive. He/she will help care for the kids and house but also be involved in the community and church. This is quite an expectation—can any of us truly live up to it? I doubt it. While a great goal, it is unrealistic.

Still, a doctor whose spouse fails to provide this shining example may begin to resent and disrespect his/her mate. Feelings of resentment, shame, and hurt appear. But it is exactly at this point that the grace of God can intervene—both spouses can draw from the deep and unconditional love of their Lord and Savior. Through forgiveness and recommunicated expectations, hearts can be knit together once again in intimacy. This ability to forgive comes through an experience of unconditional forgiveness from our Father.

Medical marriages, then, though difficult, are best started and maintained by God's grace and the spouses' mutual seeking to live in that grace.

Dispel the myths and consider the pitfalls of medical school before you begin. Your preparation will not be wasted.

Points to Ponder

1. Why is the "good day" versus the "bad day" para-digm unhealthy? What does it presuppose that is unbiblical?

2. In your own words, what is grace? Why is it important not only in term of our salvation, but to everyday life?

3. Why do you think Christians so easily forget about the role of grace in the spiritual life?

4. Tell about a time you experienced grace and how it felt.

5. Why is time such a necessary component of relationships? What makes a romantic relationship so much better when it is centered around genuine fellow-ship?

6. How would the list/GIST paradigms (see chapter 2) help us see romantic relationships in light of the gospel?

7. What difficulties would you expect in a medical marriage? How does who we are in Christ address some of

these difficulties?

8. How does our security and significance in Christ help us better love our classmates, teachers, and family? Think of some specific examples.

Notes

1. *Trends: U.S. Medical School Applicants, Mariculates and Graduates* (Washington, DC: Association of American Medical Colleges, 1995), 34.

2. Peter Brown, *Augustine of Hippo: A Biography* (Berkeley, CA: University of California Press, 1967), 101-14.

3. Jerry Bridges, *The Discipline of Grace* (Colorado Springs: NavPress, 1994), 46.

4. W. J. Doherty and S. K. Burge, "Divorce among physicians: comparison with other occupational groups," *The Journal of the American Medical Association* 261(1989):2374-7.

5. G. O. Gabbard and R. W. Menninger, "The psychology of postponement in the medical marriage," *The Journal of the American Medical Association,* 261(16) (1989):2378-81.

6. Larry Crabb, *The Marriage Builder* (Grand Rapids, MI: Zondervan, 1982), 29.

Chapter 7
The Good Doctor

A bodily disease may be but a symptom of some ailment in the spiritual past.
—Nathaniel Hawthorne

And a woman was there who had been subject to bleeding for twelve years. She had suffered a great deal under the care of many doctors and had spent all she had, yet instead of getting better she grew worse.
—Mark 5:25-26

On the very first day of orientation for first-year medical students at my medical school, there was the White Coat Ceremony. Each new medical student was called to the front during a recitation of a long and impressive list of his/her accomplishments. Upon reaching the front, the student was offered a new, crisply pressed white coat to slip on. A smile, nod, and handshake later, the student was officially christened to become "the good doctor."

After this ceremony, the dean of students asked the proud and glowing student body to describe what a good doctor is. Words like *compassionate, thoughtful, educated, capable,* and *dedicated* ensued. After an extensive and satisfactory list was compiled, the dean offered her belief that all of the students would in time reflect all of these qualities, and therefore become the "good doctors" they longed to be.

It was not until later that I realized that this was the first step down a slippery slope. The "secular" world of graduate medical education was and is prepared to inculcate within you an altogether different value system, one that, for instance, limits the role of physician to a biotechnologist. Be on guard; one might think that the medical education system is teaching only medicine when in fact it is also subtly teaching a moral value system. An article in *Academic Medicine* had this commentary:

> We argue that although matters of technical information and the transmission of technical skills traditionally have been thought to lie at the heart of the medical educational system, medical training at root is a process of moral enculturation, and that in transmitting normative rules regarding behavior and emotions to its trainees, the medical school functions as a moral community. . . . In sum, 1. students encounter an endless barrage of often conflicting messages about the nature of medical work and their place in it; 2. students internalize an appreciable number of clinically relevant values well before they formally embark on their clinical training; and 3. the overall process of medical training helps establish and reinforce a value climate that explicitly identifies

matters of rightness and wrongness within the overall culture of medicine. From these perspectives, a significant component of medical training involves the development of a medical morality and supporting rationales within its initiates.[1]

Perhaps one thinks that the graduate medical education system is valid in its traditional stance, that it is not the role of a physician to address spiritual needs, that physicians are charged with tending to biomedical needs exclusively, leaving the rest to counselors, pastors, friends, and family. Nonsense! By nature, physicians function in a quasi-priestly role. Patients look to them not only for medical advice, but for strength, hope, and wisdom. Physicians are put in positions where they are required to address whole-person needs. One will address them appropriately or inappropriately. It's as simple as that. He or she will either be a good doctor, a mediocre doctor, or a poor doctor.

What is a good doctor? A better question perhaps is, in light of a biblical worldview, *What kind of physician does God want me to be?* To be sure, there is no book or passage of the Bible pertaining directly to physicians. It is a more complicated question, then, of what the picture of a Christian physician is. To begin to answer this, let us first examine God's calling for all of His children regarding how we should treat and deal with one another.

The Good Shepherd

I hate good-byes. I never really know what to say, especially when the person has been extraordinarily meaningful in my life. I feel as if I need to use words both touching and profound. Medical-school graduation was a case in point, as I braced myself to part with several guys who walked with me through the years of school and deeply impacted my life for Christ. I thought for weeks of what I might say that would be meaningful because I loved them dearly and wanted them to know it.

Imagine the preparation and forethought of Jesus as He prepared to say good-bye to His disciples for the last time until eternity. He had predicted His death, then was promptly crucified and resurrected. For forty days, He walked with them, taught them, and encouraged them. But

Highlight #1

Traditional graduate medical education will attempt to inculcate within you what a "good doctor" is via its own set of morals.

121

the time approached of His departure. What would this gentle, loving Master say to those He loved dearly? What could He impart that He had not already imparted; what could He charge that would have an impact for a lifetime? Let's examine these important words in the last chapter of the book of John.

> This was now the third time Jesus appeared to his disciples after he was raised from the dead. When they had finished eating, Jesus said to Simon Peter, "Simon son of John, do you truly love me more than these?" "Yes, Lord," he said, "you know that I love you." Jesus said, "Feed my lambs." Again Jesus said, "Simon son of John, do you truly love me?" He answered, "Yes, Lord, you know that I love you." Jesus said, "Take care of my sheep." The third time he said to him, "Simon son of John, do you love me?" Peter was hurt because Jesus asked him the third time, "Do you love me?" He said, "Lord, you know all things; you know that I love you." Jesus said, "Feed my sheep." (John 21:14-17)

Here Jesus gently dignifies Peter by offering the opportunity to affirm his love for Jesus the same number of times he denied Him earlier. But Jesus also charges Peter with the exhortation that if he loved Him, he should show his love by taking care of His people, by tending to their needs, by directing and redirecting out of love, and by sacrificing his own life if need be. As parting words for Peter, Jesus charges him to be a good shepherd to His flock.

We too, as believers in Christ, are charged with being the good shepherd to His flock. There is nothing super-spiritual about this charge; it simply means to take care of and to address the needs of a people—God's people. Because of our unique training as physicians, we are privileged to be able to take care of and address the needs of the *whole person*. That makes physicians more than just biotechnologists, it makes them conduits of whole-person healing. To investigate this concept further let's discuss what the whole person is.

The diagram on page 123 developed by Bill Peel for *The Saline Solution* conference[2] has been helpful to me. Humans are a unique creation in that we are spiritual as

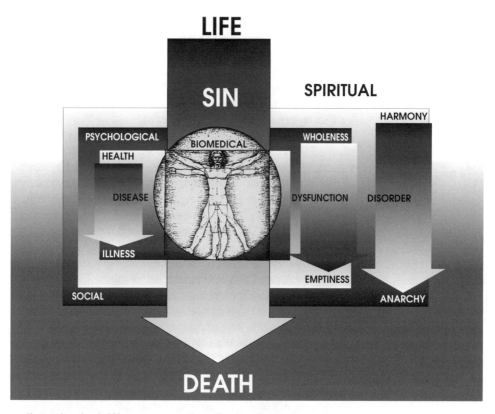

well as physical. We are more than flesh and bones (biomedical). We are also beings of mind and emotion (psychological) and community dynamics (sociological). These are all part of our God-created being. Biomedicine is only a subset of a larger system, each with interrelating pathology. To deal with any one without considering the impact on the others is futility.

Humans are complex creations; each component impacts the others. For instance, the relationship between psychological and physical pathology is well documented. The inability to cope with stress provides an illustration. This inability may lead to subclinical depression, then to full-blown clinical depression. Depression may then lead to substance abuse, which may lead to liver or heart disease. To address the biomedical needs of the patient with liver failure secondary to alcohol abuse and not address the pain and emptiness of depression is incomplete care of the whole person.

Ultimately, however, the root of the problem is spiritual in nature. The human being is born in a state of illness, emptiness, and anarchy because of the problem of sin. We are dead spiritually. We are separated from God. We lost vast portions of the benefits of living under God's kingdom when Adam and Eve decided to meet their needs in this world apart from God—and God let them (and us) feel what it's like to live separate from His care.

God told Adam and Eve that on the day they disobeyed Him they would die. This sentence was immediate spiritual death—separation from God. Adam and Eve also experienced social dysfunction for the first time as they blamed each other for sinning. They felt guilt, shame, and brokenness; no longer did they experience the oneness of perfect union in Christ. Psychological emptiness manifested itself in fear as they ran and hid from God. And though they did not die physically at the moment they sinned, biological death was and is the inevitable consequence of spiritual death. Because of sin, life for Adam and Eve transformed from wholeness, health, and harmony to illness, emptiness, and anarchy.

It is an important aside here to recognize that although God pronounced judgment, He acted toward Adam and Eve with grace and love. Almost before He finished pronouncing the curse, He made garments of skin for Adam and his wife to wear. Understand the power of this image: Adam and Eve are naked, ashamed, and guilty before God, for they have sinned by breaking the only commandment He gave them. In response God reveals the full picture of what they had done, yet provides a cloth of security, purchased by bloodshed. He procures for them covering for their nakedness, just as He will procure for them righteousness for their guilt through a sacrificial death. This is a foreshadowing of the cross of Christ. God, a benevolent God, acts lovingly toward His own.

Yet, death became part of life. The Hebrew word for death means the process by which one's physical body ceases to function and the soul departs from it. We know from the apostle Paul that all men are now faced with this mortality because of the disobedience of Adam.

> Just as sin entered the world through one man, and death through sin, and in this way death came to all men, because all sinned. (Rom. 5:12)

The Greek word for death, *thanatos*, connotes separation, not cessation. Death is not the ceasing of existence or life, but simply a separation between what was and what is. Physical death was seen as the separation of the soul from the body, the latter turning to dust. Spiritual death is also seen as a real existence but in separation from communion with God. Those who are spiritually dead (unbelievers) are not in fellowship with God; they are dead or separated from Him. So *thanatos* has a dual meaning: the physical separation of soul and body, and the spiritual separation of God and man.

Now that we have briefly examined the origins of death, let us also briefly ponder the biblical concept of health and healing. There are three words for healing in the New Testament. *Therapeuo* was usually used in the setting of physical healing.

> Jesus went throughout Galilee, teaching in their synagogues, preaching the good news of the kingdom, and healing [*therapeuo*] every disease and sickness among the people. News about him spread all over Syria, and people brought to him all who were ill with various diseases, those suffering severe pain, the demon-possessed, those having seizures, and the paralyzed, and he healed [*therapeuo*] them. (Matt. 4:23-24)

The second word for healing was *iaomai,* which has both spiritual and physical components. Twenty-two times in the New Testament it's used to mean physical healing, but it's also used figuratively to refer to spiritual healing.

> When Jesus had called the Twelve together, he gave them power and authority to drive out all demons and to cure [*iaomai*] diseases, and he sent them out to preach the kingdom of God and to heal [*iaomai*] the sick. (Luke 9:1-2)

> He has blinded their eyes and deadened their hearts, so they can neither see with their eyes, nor understand with their hearts, nor turn—and I would heal [*iaomai*] them. (John 12:40)

Sozo is the final word for healing in the New Testament. It is translated "to save, to make whole" and it refers

Highlight #2

God uses Christian physicians to heal physically, psychologically, socially, and spiritually— whole-person healing.

to the whole person. It is the concept of saving from death, disease, and their effects on the entire individual. Let us read a passage where there was first *ioamai* healing and then *sozo* healing and observe the difference:

> Ten men who had leprosy met him. They stood at a distance and called out in a loud voice, "Jesus, Master, have pity on us!" When he saw them, he said, "Go, show yourselves to the priests." And as they went, they were cleansed. One of them, when he saw he was healed [*ioamai*], came back, praising God in a loud voice. He threw himself at Jesus' feet and thanked him—and he was a Samaritan. Jesus asked, "Were not all ten cleansed? Where are the other nine? Was no one found to return and give praise to God except this foreigner?" Then he said to him, "Rise and go; your faith has made you well [*sozo*]." (Luke 17:12-19)

It was this gentile, likely a nonbeliever, who was healed physically of his leprosy (*iaomai*). And it was this Samaritan who was made whole on the inside as he recognized the Messiah sent from God, giving thanks in his heart for mercy and grace (*sozo*). He was saved, preserved, made whole inside and out. This is the complete healing of the ministry of the Great Physician.

The Good Shepherd and Whole-person Healing

Restoration of spiritual health can be accomplished only by dealing with the problem of sin, and the sin problem can be dealt with only by regeneration and redemption. God offers these as the solution to sin and thus offers health, wholeness, harmony, and life to each person. One may say, "This sounds all well and good, but isn't it just esoteric theology? How is this translated to daily living in the doctor-patient relationship?" Let me use two cases to illustrate.

The first patient, "Gordon," has been a successful attorney for the past forty years and has lived what most people would call a full life: he has a three-story house in the richest part of town, a six-figure income, a lovely wife, and three beautiful and successful children. Everyone who knows Gordon says that he is larger than life, that he always seems to be a winner in everything he does. Gordon "has it together." Then he notices some blood in his stools, and that he has lost considerable weight in the past six months. And he's had a dull abdominal pain. After a battery of diagnostic tests, Gordon's doctor tells him that he has widespread colon cancer and about six months to live. The doctor elaborates on trial drugs that may increase survival a few months, but Gordon does not really hear him. Gordon just thinks, *I know why I am dying medically, but why do I have to die?* Gordon now must wrestle as never before with the basic existentialist questions: Who am I and where am I going?

"Cindy" is a fifteen-year-old girl from a severely dysfunctional home. Her mother is an alcoholic and her father is in jail. She has been in several romantic relationships recently in a desperate attempt to find approval and security; each was short-lived and unsatisfying. She goes to see her gynecologist for a follow-up exam, since she was in the office several months ago because of discharge and pain. At that time Cindy's doctor prescribed antibiotics, performed a pap smear and physical exam, and said she would be in touch. The pap smear showed cells that were suspicious for a type of viral infection. On today's visit, Cindy reports that she has been feeling ill lately. She reveals that she missed her last period, and her doctor performs a quick pregnancy test—which is positive. Cindy is horrified, saying she doesn't even know who is the father. She is sure her life is over.

In both instances, the patient has physical, psychological, social, and spiritual needs. Most physicians, however, are taught to expeditiously sift through the physical needs and address them accordingly, allowing the spiritual needs to be resolved later, perhaps on the patient's own. This is not the ministry of healing of the good shepherd. The good shepherd recognizes that Gordon and Cindy are people with needs even more distressing than their physical ones. He/she is called to address those needs as well. While we may not explain the gospel to every patient, we will treat even "illnesses" that aren't physical as best we can. Being the good shepherd may mean comforting—placing a hand on Gordon's shoulder and bringing dignity to his pain by acknowledging it. It may mean discussing how his prognosis affects his view of life and death. Being the good shepherd might mean wrapping your arms around Cindy and letting her know that even if no one is around to walk with her through this trial, you are, and then following through with it. Or it might mean referring her to someone else who has the time and expertise to help her during this very difficult time. In either case, being the good shepherd may mean revealing the One in whom real and unconditional approval and security can be found. And of course, being the good shepherd involves prescribing any physical treatment: chemotherapy, pain killers, antibiotics, and/or prenatal care that may be necessary.

Qualities of a Good Shepherd

It is one thing to read about being a good shepherd to God's flock; it is quite another thing to practice it. What are some principles and guidelines to follow? Bill Peel, director of the Paul Tournier Institute, suggests that there are four key ingredients to spiritual influence[3]:

Quality 1
Professional Competence

There are two reasons why competence is important. First, excellence is a standard set by God for His people. Ecclesiastes 9:10 says, "Whatever your hand finds to do, do it with all your might." Colossians 3:23 underscores this command: "Whatever you do, work at it with all your heart, as working for the Lord, not for men." Jesus Christ requires us, whatever our profession might be, to do our work with excellence because it is for Him and He deserves our best.

Second, excellence is a strategy. If we want to be doctors who have spiritual influence on our patients, we cannot sidestep excellence. Says Peel, "People do not care if we are good people until they know that we are good doctors. If we want people to pay attention to our faith, we must first pay attention to our work." This excellence may take the form of being up-to-date on the latest drugs and procedures, being careful and thorough in the history taking, physical examination, and all subsequent tests, and taking the time to find out answers to questions that a patient may have. A patient of mine summed it up well just hours before his surgery when he said, "If I had to choose between competence and compassion, right now I'd choose competence!" Patients desire and deserve our excellence as we strive to work for the Lord.

Quality 2
Character

Galatians 5:22-23 says, "The fruit of the Spirit is love, joy, peace, patience, kindness, goodness, faithfulness, gentleness, and self-control. Against such things there is no law." The evidence of a godly spiritual life is Christlikeness. This character is admired everywhere. When people see love, joy, peace, and patience in a person, they are drawn to it. That kind of character attracts people even if they disagree with what you believe.

The key question that we need to ask ourselves as we go through the day dealing with character issues is, "What would Jesus do? How would He respond to this situation?" Dr. John Leonard, the chief of house staff for internal medicine at Vanderbilt University, tells his residents and students that there are four key components to Christian character in a physician.

1. Christian physicians are impartial. Just as the Good Samaritan was impartial in taking care of the injured Jew, so should physicians be impartial in taking care of the poor and sick. Some patients are simply harder to take care of because of their self-destructive habits, upbringing, culture, and even hygiene. But Jesus wants us to bring excellent care to all those we encounter.

2. Christian physicians are humble. It is important to see that God is the healer of all and that we are simply conduits in this process. Physicians should lay aside the accouterments of being a physician and become servants like Jesus. This means we are not above menial tasks, as Jesus was not above washing His disciples' feet. Physicians should model their practice after the Great Physician who Himself gave up all to become a servant to all.

3. Christian physicians are faithful. There are subtle ways in which physicians can abandon their patients. Sometimes they're simply not present at crucial moments. Or they might fail to fully investigate a problem, leaving it to be solved later or not at all. Or they might be too careless to provide hope and strength when it is

Highlight #3

The four qualities of a good physician are competence, character, compassion, and communication.

129

necessary. Knowing that God is faithful to His children even when they are not faithful to Him, physicians should strive to be faithful to their patients.

4. Christian physicians are honest. It is easy to gloss over the truth in dealing with a patient and his/her family. These people put a great deal of trust in their caregivers and will believe what they're told. Therefore, it is imperative that physicians be totally honest with the patient and the patient's family.

Quality 3
Compassion

Compassion is the logical result of experiencing grace. If we ever find ourselves lacking compassion, it is because we have lost the sense of God's graciousness to us. Compassion involves our speech—Ephesians 4:29 tells us, "Do not let any unwholesome talk come out of your mouths, but only what is helpful for building others up according to their needs." And compassion involves our action—"Do nothing out of selfish ambition," said Paul in Philippians 2:3.

In most instances, compassion will take the form of comforting our patients. We read in 2 Corinthians:

Praise be to the God and Father of our Lord Jesus Christ, the Father of compassion and the God of all comfort, who comforts us in all our troubles, so that we can comfort those in any trouble with the comfort we ourselves have received from God. (2 Cor. 1:3-4)

For physicians, comforting means lending strength to patients, coming alongside them to provide help from the comfort we ourselves have received from God. It means bringing love to our patients out of the love we have received from God. Compassion springs from our hearts inasmuch as we have received and experienced compassion from God.

Quality 4
Communication

In the process of making a spiritual impact on patients we must learn how to overcome emotional obstacles by

communicating words of hope in words they can understand (again, avoid Christianese). People want words of
encouragement, not necessarily detailed answers or
explanations.

Far from reluctant, most patients want their doctors to
initiate conversation about faith. This flies in the face of the
traditional medical education that taught doctors were
never to talk about faith issues with their patients. Given
the importance of faith to most Americans it's not surprising
that more than 75 percent of patients surveyed believed
their physicians should address spiritual issues as part of
their medical care. Nearly one in two patients wanted his
doctor to pray with him.[4]

The Faith Flag

One of the simplest tools for beginning to cultivate the hard
ground of the heart is a "faith flag." A faith flag is a brief
statement in the course of a natural conversation in which
one identifies him- or herself as someone to whom the
Bible, prayer, or God (not church or denominations—
they're subjects too problematic for many people) is
important.

What are some principles in raising faith flags? First
of all, they should occur as a natural part of conversation.
When asked to list fifteen or twenty sample faith flags, Dr.
Walt Larimore, a gifted evangelist and family physician in
Kissimmee, Florida, said, "I can't. They are not contrived;
they're not made up; they're not rehearsed. They just
happen as part of a conversation. Remember that I've
already started that day off spending some time with the
Lord. I've already talked with Him. I've already tried to
center my life on Him. I've already tried to get Him to fill,
control, and empower me and I look at each appointment
through that day as a divine appointment. My nurse and I
have bathed that particular half-day in prayer, and then I
walk into each room with expectancy, trying to find out what
God is doing. With that type of expectancy, faith flags
become a natural part of conversation."[5]

Faith flags take no more than a few seconds and, in
fact, if they take longer, they are not faith flags. Most of my
faith flags last five, ten, or fifteen seconds. Be careful not to
confuse giving a faith flag with giving a sermon. Even if a
patient indicates interest in what I have said, I usually let

Highlight #4

*A faith flag is a
brief statement in
the course of a
natural
conversation in
which a doctor
identifies him- or
herself as a
person who
believes in the
Bible, prayer, or
God.*

the flag "rest" for a time and follow up later. This communicates that Christians are not "hounds out on a chase." If, however, it feels very natural to transition onto a spiritual topic, then I do so. It is important to understand that faith flags do not demand a response. Sometimes the comments seem to make no impact at all; other times the patient's eyes light up. The more faith flags we raise and the more opportunities we give God's Spirit to communicate through us, the more results we see—as long as we're lifting our flags in the manner and timing of His direction.

Highlight #5

Faith stories tell how God or a biblical principle became real in someone's life—preferably yours—and are a natural part of conversation, not contrived.

Here are a few examples:

- I remember the first time I heard what the Bible had to say about being discouraged. Maybe we can talk more about that sometime.
- I know you are having difficulty dealing with this illness. Would it be okay if I prayed for you?
- Do you know anyone who can pray for you as you are recovering?

Faith Stories

There may come a time when, as a natural part of conversation, it is appropriate to share a faith story. A faith story tells how God or a biblical principle became real in your life. (A faith flag may refer to a faith story, but they are not the same. Faith flags are too brief to be faith stories—they just hint at them.) A faith story can come from anyone's life, but they are most effective when they come from yours. Much like faith flags, they should fit smoothly into the conversation and not be forced or contrived. You should avoid religious jargon and pushing for a decision. Words are only a small part of communication and in themselves are powerless, but when the Spirit works with our words, the message of life is revealed. We should be confident in sharing our faith because God's Spirit communicates through us. Therefore, neither the delivery nor the result is left to us alone. God is with us.

One may respond that the use of faith flags and faith stories is too much of a laissez-faire approach to evangelism. I used to think so too, until I learned a very important lesson about the spiritual life: we cannot force fruit. We simply cannot promote maturity before it is time. No matter how badly we want to grow or see others grow, we cannot make it happen outside of the time line of God. And bet that God does have a time line where there is no rush to finish. Earlier we read Paul's words to the Philippians, "He who began a good work in you will carry it on to completion until the day of Christ Jesus" (Phil. 1:6). And it will take exactly that long too! Don't worry.

> Consider the ravens: They do not sow or reap, they have no storeroom or barn; yet God feeds them. And how much valuable you are than birds! Who of you by worrying can add a single hour to his life? Since you cannot do this very little thing, why do you worry about the rest? Consider how the lilies grow. They do not labor or spin. Yet I tell you, not even Solomon in all his splendor was dressed like one of these. If that is how God clothes the grass of the field, which is here today, and tomorrow is thrown into the fire, how much more will he clothe you, O you of little faith! And do not set your heart on what you will eat or drink; do not worry about it. For the pagan world runs after all such things, and your Father knows that you need them. But seek his kingdom, and these things will be given to you as well. Do not be afraid, little flock, for your Father has been pleased to give you the king-dom. (Luke 12:24-32)

Highlight #6

One cannot preempt God's timing for spiritual maturity. Fruit cannot be forced.

The Father has gladly given us the kingdom. The kingdom keys are ours—yet we worry about spiritual growth! Cultivation of the spiritual life is a lifelong process. Life is made abundant, but according to God's timing. We cannot rush it nor can we stop it. God is the giver of life and He has given it to us abundantly. But it takes time for it to become a living reality in our lives. We should therefore understand that the shepherding of God's flock does not include pushing, forcing, or manipulating people into a decision. Life will replicate, but on God's preprogrammed schedule. This is a principle called *sovereignty*. J. I. Packer puts it this way:

> This confidence should make us patient. It should keep us from being daunted when we find that our evangelistic endeavors meet with no immediate response. God saves in His own time, and we ought

not to suppose that He is in a hurry as we are. We need to remember that we are all children of our age, and the spirit of our age is a spirit of tearing hurry. And it is a pragmatic spirit; it is a spirit that demands quick results. The modern ideal is to achieve more and more by doing less and less. This is the age of the labour-saving device, the efficiency chart, and automatism. . . . The truth is that the work of evangelism takes more patience and sheer "stickability," more reserves of persevering love and care, than most of us twentieth-century Christians have at command. . . . As He kept Abraham waiting twenty-five years for the birth of a son, so He often keeps Christians waiting for things that they long to see, such as the conversion of their friends. We need patience, then, if we are do to our part in helping others towards faith. And the way for us to develop that patience is to learn to live in terms of our knowledge of the free and gracious sovereignty of God.[5]

Highlight #7

Research has consistently shown a relationship between spirituality and health.

The Medical Effects of Spirituality

It is encouraging to note that scientific groups studying the clinical effects of spirituality have found an undeniable relationship between good health and religious commitment. Levin and Schiller reviewed 250 studies regarding the relationship of religious commitment and the incidence of cardiovascular disease, hypertension, stroke, colitis, enteritis, general-health status, general mortality, cancer of the uterus and cervix, and other nonuterine cancers. They consistently found positive associations between religious commitment and physical health for these disorders.[7] Oxman *et al* studied factors that best predict survival from cardiac surgery and found religious commitment and participation in social groups to both have positive effects on survival. Of the thirty-seven patients who described themselves as deeply religious, none had died at the six-month follow-up whereas the 4 percent engaged in organized groups (local government, senior center, historical society) and the 14 percent uninvolved in any groups had died.[8] Those who found strength in their faith were associated with lower levels of depressive symptoms and better ambulation status after surgical repair of hips.[9] In another study, Larson *et al* found that faith correlated positively with a lower diastolic blood pressure.[10] And the studies go on.

It is truth and it does work. Let us not be fooled by the rhetoric of this world and of secular graduate medical education that teaches us to stick to biomechanics, but instead search diligently through Scripture to learn what a "good doctor" is by understanding the qualities of a "good shepherd," serving and protecting those around us. Let us do so with competency, character, compassion, and good communication skills. Let us be committed to being used by God as a conduit of whole-person healing—physical, psychological, social, and spiritual. Let us recognize that although all individuals must die physically as a result of sin and the curse, that we as good doctors may know in our hearts and speak in our actions that Jesus has come "that they may have life, and have it to the full" (John 10:10). Ponder with me, for a lifetime, who this "Gentle Healer" is as described by the writer and musician Michael Card.

> The gentle healer came into our town today;
> He touched blind eyes and their darkness left to stay;
> But more than the blindness, He took their sins away;
> The gentle healer came into our town today.
>
> The gentle healer came into our town today;
> He spoke one word that was all He had to say;
> And the one who had died just rose up straight away;
> The gentle healer came into our town today.
>
> Oh, He seems like just an ordinary man;
> With dirty feet and rough but gentle hands;
> But the words He says are hard to understand;
> And yet he seems like just an ordinary man.
>
> The gentle healer, He left our town today;
> I just looked around and found He'd gone away;
> Some folks from town followed Him, they say:
> That the Gentle Healer is the truth, the life, the way.[11]

Points to Ponder

1. How are all of us asked to be "shepherds" to God's people, as Peter was?

2. Using the diagram on page 123, describe specific

examples of pathology of each component humans have: biomedical, psychological, sociological, and spiritual (i.e., pneumonia causes physical health to change to illness).

3. Considering Genesis 2 and 3, explain why it is inaccurate to say grace is a function only revealed in the New Testament.

4. Read the following passages and decide which type of healing Jesus performed (*therapeuo, iaomai, sozo*): Matthew 14:14, Luke 5:17-20, Matthew 9:20-22.

5. Using the characters of Gordon and Cindy, diagnose the physical, psychological, sociological, and spiritual issues that must be dealt with.

6. Of the four qualities of a good shepherd, which one or two do you think God has most gifted you with?

7. Think of some faith flags you have raised in recent conversations and share them with the group. Do the same with faith stories.

8. What is standing in your way to use faith flags and faith stories today, even as a premed student?

9. Does it surprise you that research has consistently shown a relationship between spirituality and physical health? How might you relay this to your colleagues, friends, and patients?

Notes

1. F. W. Hafferty and R. Franks, "The hidden curriculum, ethics teaching and the structure of medical education," *Academic Medicine* 11 (1994):861-71.

2. W. L. Larimore and W. C. Peel, *The Saline Solution* Workbook, The Christian Medical and Dental Society, Bristol, TN, 1996), 5.

3. Unpublished notes from W. L. Larimore and W. C. Peel, *The Saline Solution* Conference, The Christian Medical and Dental Society, Bristol, TN, 1996.

4. D. E. King and B. Bushwick, "Beliefs and attitudes of hospital inpatients about faith and prayer," *Journal of Family Practice,* 39(4) (1994):349-352.

5. W. L. Larimore and W. C. Peel, *The Saline Solution.*

6. J. I. Packer, *Evangelism and the Sovereignty of God* (Downers Grove, IL: InterVarsity Press, 1991), 119-121.

7. J.S. Levin and F.L. Schiller, "Is there a religious

factor in health?" *Journal of Religion and Health,* 26 (1987):9-35.

8. T. E. Oxman, P. H. Freeman, Jr., E.D. Manheimer, "Lack of social participation or religious strength and comfort as risk factors for death after cardiac surgery in the elderly," *Psychosomatic Medicine,* 57(1) (1996): 5-15.

9. P. Pressman, J. S. Lyons, D. B. Larson, and J. J. Strain. "Religious belief, depression and ambulation status in elderly women with broken hips," *American Journal of Psychiatry,* 147 (1990):758-60.

10. D. B. Larson, H. G. Koening, B. H. Kaplan, R. S. Greenberg, E. Logue, and H. A. Tyroler, "The impact of religion on men's blood pressure," *Journal of Religion and Health,* 4 (1989):265-278.

11. Michael Card, "The Gentle Healer" © 1986 Birdwing Music/Mole End Music. All rights reserved. Used by permission.

Appendix

Of making many books there is no end, and much study wearies the body.
—Ecclesiastes 12:12

"For I know the plans I have for you," declares the Lord, "plans to prosper you and not to harm you, plans to give you hope and a future."
—Jeremiah 29:11

T his is a list of valuable resources that I highly recommend. It is an admixture of organizations, conferences, books/reference materials, and programs that I hope you will find useful and enriching.

Christian Medical and Dental Society-Premed

Christians are the salt of the earth. College campuses need the ministry and influence of individual Christians and of organizations dedicated to Christ. The following are a few of the needs that an organized ministry like CMDS-Premed can uniquely fulfill.

CMDS helps prepare Christian premed students for their profession. There are several dimensions in which premed students must be prepared for medical school and for their eventual medical practice. A college education provides the intellectual development needed for the success of the medical student, but it cannot begin to address the increasingly difficult spiritual issues facing those involved in the medical profession in our modern society. Amidst the plethora of secular approaches to medicine today, Christian premed students need to be firmly grounded in biblical truths, and they must be sharpened spiritually so that they will be ready to practically apply this knowledge to the issues they will face as medical doctors. CMDS-Premed exists to provide this encouragement and "to equip the saints for the work of service."

CMDS provides fellowship. Those who develop spiritually rarely do so alone. Spiritual growth requires the mutual sharpening and encouragement that takes place between believers who are united in mind and spirit. CMDS-Premed provides opportunities for Christian premed students to share together in ministry, in Bible study, in prayer, and in enjoyable fellowship. When students with common goals and objectives participate together in these activities, spiritual growth results.

CMDS provides opportunities to witness for Jesus Christ. College campuses are open mission fields full of students who need to hear the good news of Jesus Christ. Many Christians are unable to find an outlet for ministry suitable to their talents and interests. Members of CMDS-Premed are given opportunities to lift up Jesus Christ by being godly witnesses and sharing their testimonies with their peers. Monthly Forums are vehicles by which speakers are able to share Christ with large numbers of students and open doors for one-on-one follow-up sharing and testimony. Other outreaches, such visiting nursing-home patients, feeding the poor, or traveling abroad for summer mission trips, provide opportunities to be witnesses for Christ by demonstrating His love. In this way, God willing, committed students will win souls for Christ and advance His kingdom in the world.

If you have any questions about this organization or about spearheading and founding a premed chapter on your campus, please contact:

Christian Medical and Dental Society
P.O. Box 7500
Bristol, TN 37621-0005

PHONE: (888) 690-9054 or (423) 844-1000
FAX (423) 844-1005
EMAIL: main@christian-doctors.com

CMDS can mail you a packet of information and give you references and names of individuals who will be willing to assist you in this process.

Medical Group Missions and Global Health Outreach

This ministry of CMDS is committed to bringing healthcare and the gospel of Jesus Christ to the world. An overseas short-term missions experience is an opportunity for God to create a lasting vision in your heart. It may ignite or reignite a fire to serve God. If you want more information, contact CMDS at the number above.

Life and Health Resources

Life and Health Resources is a CMDS organization through which you can purchase a number of books and tapes at discount prices that address specific healthcare issues. To get a catalog of resources, call (888) 231-2637.

National Institutes of Healthcare Research

NIHR is composed of physicians and scientists committed to observing and documenting scientifically the relationship between faith and health. I referred to some of their work in chapter 7. For more information, call (301) 984-7162.

The Saline Solution
Materials and Conferences

The concept of the faith flag and faith story are used and taught in much greater detail in these materials and conferences. Walt Larimore, M.D. and William C. Peel, Th.M., Director of the Paul Tournier Institute, created *The Saline Solution* materials and help equip students and physicians to more effectively and comfortably share Christ and disciple patients. For more information, contact CMDS.